THE HERO'S JOURNEY TO FINANCIAL INDEPENDENCE

WILLIAM RADFORD

Published by Ropeswing Publishing

Radford, William, 1970—

The Hero's Journey to Financial Independence

Includes bibliographical references

Categories

Business & Investing

    Business Life

    Investing

    Small Business & Entrepreneurship

    Personal Finance

Health, Mind & Body

    Success

    Personal Transformation

Includes bibliographical references.

*This book is dedicated to the
people who make my life
worthwhile*

Susanne, Madison and Helena

—WR

Disclaimer

The information provided in this book is designed to provide helpful information on the subjects discussed. It is the intention of neither the author nor publisher of this book to render any type of psychological, legal, financial, medical or any other kind of professional advice. Neither the publisher nor the author shall be liable for any physical, psychological, emotional, financial, or commercial damages, including, but not limited to, special, incidental, consequential or other damages. You are responsible for your own choices, actions, and subsequent results. Choose wisely.

Contents

Introduction

There is nothing new in this book.

If this is bothersome to you I suggest kindly returning it to the shelf and looking elsewhere. If you have already purchased this as an e-book or from an online bookseller then I insist that you demand a refund. There are plenty of books with *new* ideas on ways to achieve financial independence out there. This is not one of them. Some of them have very slick covers and are quite thick. A great cover and several hundred pages probably means they are chock full of great information, right? *Perhaps*.

My goal in writing this book is to provide a practical, step by step guide to achieving financial independence. My sincere wish is that a unique way of presenting *rock solid financial fundamentals* will inspire you to launch a journey of your own.

The ideas presented in this book are very old and have withstood the test of time. They just work. Just like antiques and fine wine, great financial ideas have a strong and enduring history. There are no new **old** ideas. You would call a newly manufactured antique a scam and you should be equally wary of new financial concepts. Granted, some new ideas will eventually live on to be grand old nuggets of financial wisdom but most will wither and die and be forgotten to all but the unfortunate people who acted on them.

What is different here is the context in which these timeless ideas are presented. There are no secrets or magic formulas involved in achieving financial independence. The hardest part is cutting through the misinformation that surrounds so much of our financial lives. When we jettison the junk regarding money and wealth, we are left with just a few gems.

While I am proud of the cover art (I did it myself, what do you think?), I am equally proud of the brevity of this book. I worked hard to create a small volume that is interesting, factual and informative. The hardest part is to decide what to leave out. Strunk and White's classic book on grammar, **The Elements of Style**, taught us to 'omit needless words'. Too often a books page count is artificially bloated in order to achieve a marketing goal. Publishers fear that too few pages will affect the perception of quality. They urge the author to hit that magic 2-300 page range when the ideas could have been persuasively presented in a fraction of that. In my experience, books that are unwieldy and full of filler rarely get finished. A book you don't read will do you no good. To that end I have taken it as my responsibility to *omit needless words* from this book.

The concept is based in part on the combined works of Joseph Campbell, especially **The Hero with a Thousand Faces** (Campbell, 1949). In it he describes a series of steps common to thousands of mythological tales from around the world and throughout time. This is the hero's journey or monomyth. He found that the great stories shared a common core and that the stories of the hero are the story of us. Our shared heritage that makes us all the same is also the mechanism that allows us to express our uniqueness. Everyone's life carries within it the seed of the entire hero journey. This feat is not reserved for a Perseus or a Hercules. It is in fact the entire pantheon of gods and human heroes that serve as a model for our own departure, initiation and return. The faces of all heroes appear unique but are in fact the same. By approaching these topics with the eyes of an anthropologist, he exposes amazing similarities between cultures that could not, on the surface, seem more distant. His examples range from the Buddha of the Far East to the Spider Woman of indigenous North America; from the warrior Finn McCool of Ireland to the Jains of India.

While heavily influenced by the psychologist Carl Jung, The philosopher Friedrich Nietzsche and the novelist James Joyce, Campbell developed his own powerful, original voice.

Another of Campbell's major influences was the anthropologist Adolph Bastian. Bastian first ignited the idea that myths from all over the world and from various times were assembled from the same building blocks. He called these the **elementary ideas** which became a major influence in the concept of the monomyth.

Whether it is the Greek account of Odysseus or the Norse tale of Odin, these stories carry within them the seed of the human condition. They speak to us at a level far deeper than our consciousness. The mythological path of the hero is both entertainment and an internal guide past the thresholds we all face in our lives. A thousand faces from a thousand heroes becomes a single, abiding hero archetype in Campbell's expert hands.

We can view our personal development through the lens of this philosophy. We can look at our finances, our career and the immense challenges we face in the modern world not as unique to us, here and now, but common to the history of human experience.

Joseph Campbell's insights have stood the test of time, The Hero with a Thousand Faces was first published in 1949 and countless books, screenplays and stories have used the hero's journey as inspiration and guide. George Lucas borrowed Campbell's richly formed character archetypes and classical narrative structure for his **Star Wars** series. Many scholars agree that the wildly popular **Harry Potter** books track very closely to the monomyth structure, an observation J.K. Rowling has yet to confirm. Christopher Vogler's screenplay writing guide, **The Writers Journey** and the great works it has spawned is evidence of the profound impact mythological story has on the human mind.

The struggles of the mythical hero help us understand the very real trials we go through in our own lives. It is a fallacy to think that all of our problems and all of our challenges are unique to present day concerns. Just about every challenge we face in our modern life our ancestors once had to pass. The background may have changed but the thresholds are the same.

> *"A hero is someone who has given his or her life to something bigger than oneself."*
>
> **—Joseph Campbell**

The Hero's Journey to Financial Independence is intended to help you deal with your money in a way that serves you best. While mythology and ritual set the stage for this discussion, the financial ideas are rock-solid and thoroughly tested.

It is fitting to begin with one of the many pearls of wisdom that Joseph Campbell brought to us from his personal journey. These words really do hold the secret to achieving financial freedom and personal fulfillment.

> *"Follow your bliss."*
>
> **—Joseph Campbell**

The Ordinary World

The Ordinary World is the launching point of our personal story. Technically speaking, this is the hero's normal world before the story even begins.

"In a hole in the ground there lived a hobbit. Not a nasty, dirty, wet hole, filled with the ends of worms and an oozy smell, nor yet a dry, bare, sandy hole with nothing in it to sit down on or to eat: it was a hobbit-hole, and that means comfort."

— J.R.R. Tolkien (The Hobbit)

This is home. Being home in both physical and figurative terms is possibly the most comforting place of all. This presents a bit of a dilemma. When we are away for long we pine for home but if we spend too much time at home we crave something different. It is a battle of opposites. The more comfort we seek, the more boredom we get. Prolonged comfort should not be our outcome. A comfortable life at home is only enriched by our *journey into* and our *return from* the unknown.

It is a bit of a **Catch-22**. In order to provide for our families and live comfortably we must exit our easy chair and head off into the unknown. Our joy and fulfillment sits somewhere between our need for comfort and our thirst for adventure.

Financial Independence

As you can guess, I firmly believe one of your goals should be financial independence. Not only is becoming financially independent a worthy goal but it is also completely attainable by just about anyone. You do not need to be a high earner to get there; even a modest income, *spent lightly* and *invested wisely* is enough of a vehicle for you to achieve this. What is financial independence anyway? Here is an excellent definition:

Financial independence is the diligent conversion of work into passive income.

Passive income is made up of profits that flow to you from systems that you set up over time. These systems can be investments, products or services. With financial independence as a goal, you are able to better identify opportunities that will serve this purpose. Investing a small portion of your income each month into the free enterprise system is perhaps the best way to generate passive income. Another way is to become so good at what you are passionate about, people will pay for your service, buy your product, attend your course and seek your knowledge. You are not limited to just one. Over time you can develop multiple streams of passive income. We'll deal with the *how to* in a bit. At this point it is important to understand the *why to*.

Why would you want to be financially independent? One great reason is that financial independence means **freedom**. Freedom is the ability to do what you want, when you want to do it. Being financially free means knowing that you can change course at any time in your life. It is about having choices. When it comes down to it, *choice is better than no choice*. Self-imposed financial constraints artificially limit you. Having sufficient financial resources in place gives you room to breathe and can help you make better choices.

Being financially free is not the same as being rich or being happy. There are plenty of rich people who are made miserable by their relationship with money and their habitual choices. Money is money and happiness is happiness. Above a very moderate amount, money ceases to affect happiness. As Princeton University economist Daniel Kahneman and psychologist Angus Deaton found when evaluating thousands of poll results, there is a relationship between money and well-being but not as strong as one would think. In their report, High income improves evaluation of life but not emotional well-being (Kahneman & Deaton, 2010); they found that the magic income level for happiness was $75,000.

Happiness comes from more unlikely places. Delaying purchases and living frugally builds our willpower muscle. Yes, you read that right, our willpower can be built up through training. In **Willpower: Rediscovering the Greatest Human Strength**, authors Roy Baumeister and John Tierney uncover the science of self-control (Baumeister & Tierney, 2011). As you will learn, it is self-control, not money that brings the most enduring happiness.

First Things First

To get where we are going we need to know where we are. The best way to know where we are financially is to create our **personal balance sheet**. A balance sheet is just a snapshot of how we are doing. Its value is in providing us an accurate picture of our current financial health.

Exercise

Create Your Personal Balance Sheet

Step 1: List all of your assets:

Using a sheet of paper (You could do this on a spreadsheet or better yet with good personal finance software. I like Ace Money and YNAB as low cost, full featured applications. GNU cash is an excellent open source/free alternative. Try them out.) List the value, in dollars of all of your assets down one column. Your **assets** are just the stuff you own. Include your car, bike, toy collection, clothes. Include money in the bank, in your pocket, in a jar or in a retirement account. *If it has a value, list it.*

Step 2: List all of your liabilities: In a second column list the money you owe to other people or businesses. List your mortgage, car note, credit card debt, sister, neighbor, etc. **Any** money you owe to **any entity** goes here.

Step 3: Add up both columns: You'll come up with a 'net assets' total and a 'net liabilities' total.

Step 4: Calculate: Subtract your net liabilities from your net assets. This is your net worth:

Assets — Liabilities = Net Worth

Oh, Where Does My Cash Flow?

The next step is to evaluate your current spending habits. This is the answer to the question: **What does it cost to be me?** Understanding where our money goes is critical. It is amazing how quickly our money seems to disappear when we are not careful. Developing a financial independence plan needs to be based on habits of spending you currently have.

Track every dime you spend for several weeks. There are some excellent tools now to help you with this. **YNAB (You Need A Budget)** is my favorite. In addition to the full desktop application, they have apps for Android and iPhone so you can keep track of things on the go.

YNAB is more than just expense software it is a financial philosophy. YNAB provides an excellent comprehensive plan to help you get out of debt and stop living paycheck to paycheck if that is where you find yourself. Check out YouNeedABudget.com for more information.

You can also do this fairly effectively with just a spreadsheet, a small spiral notebook and a pencil. Write down every expense and save every receipt. When you get home plug the numbers into categories. Here are some commonly used categories. Add others that work for you. If you spend money on something, make it a category. Here are a few examples:

> Housing
> Automobile
> Food
> Insurance
> Debt Repayment
> Entertainment
> Clothing
> Medical/Dental
> Childcare

Try to avoid the *miscellaneous* category. It is easy to hide a problem by dropping it into this bucket. It is useful to create sub-categories as well. Automobile might have gas and repairs as sub-categories. The important thing to do is to account for every penny, write down every expense. This will help you determine where the money really goes and how you can change things.

You Are Not Your Brain

What we do is largely a function of our habits, **good habits** and **bad habits**. Installing habits that serve us is critical to success. A well-established positive habit can pull you through the toughest times, the darkest days.

"Nobody Likes Practice, but what's worse: Practicing, or sucking at something?...Oh, give me a f**king break, practicing is not worse than sucking."

—Justin Halpern (from the book, Sh*t My Dad Says)

It takes practice and commitment to bring an activity into the realm of habit. If you have a bad habit think of it as proof that your brain is somewhat skilled at establishing one. Identifying bad habits and deciding on positive habits to replace them is easy. Warren Buffet, one of the most successful investors in history, has been overheard reciting this quote on the subject of habits:

"Chains of habit are too weak to be felt until they are too heavy to be broken."

—Samuel Johnson

Bad habits have a tendency to creep up on you while good habits need to be intentional. How long does it take to break a bad habit? **Just one second.** It sometimes takes months or years to **not** change a habit but once you make a true decision to change, you have changed. Ex-smokers know this, so does anyone who has successfully quit anything they found destructive. It is said it takes around 21 days to establish a new habit and science seems to bear this out. The neural pathways that control both the mental and physical behaviors that accompany any habit strengthen with repeated use. You can accelerate this process through the use of variable personal rewards. Do something nice and healthy for yourself periodically while you are establishing the new habit. If I had to sum up the entire journey in just a few words it would read:

> ***The key to financial independence is replacing the habits that harm you with habits and rituals that serve your purpose.***

Dr. Jeffrey Schwartz spent years at UCLA doing research on neuro-plasticity and obsessive-compulsive disorder (OCD) treatment. In his book, ***You Are Not Your Brain, The 4 Step Solution*** (Schwartz, 2011) he outlines how you can change any behavior. Self-directed neuroplasticity is just a fancy way of saying **you can change your brain.** I highly recommend reading this book and learning the 4 steps he describes. These steps were originally developed by Dr. Schwartz to help people with OCD but are useful for just about any area of your life. OCD can be thought of as *habits in overdrive.*

Using the example of a compulsive shopper, here are the steps:

Step 1: **<u>Relabel</u>** the deceptive brain message by calling it what it really is. "*Oh, I have the urge to go buy something.*"

Step 2: **<u>Reframe</u>** your perception of the importance of the brain message: "I have the urge to shop because it feels good but I do not have to respond to every urge"

Step 3: **<u>Refocus</u>** on a good, healthy activity. "*I'll go for a walk instead.*"

Step 4: **<u>Revalue</u>** the message for what it is: "This urge to shop is nothing more than a deceptive brain message. I don't really need anything new right now so this urge is of little value."

Competence

One of the most enduring models that highlight the power of habits and rituals are Abraham Maslow's four stages of learning. In any endeavor, following the path from novice to expert takes focus, discipline and effort. There are four stages that are recognized as the steps one goes through to gain mastery in any area.

Stage 1: Unconscious incompetence: The person does not know how to do something and does not even recognize it as a problem.

Stage 2: Conscious incompetence: The person still does not know how to do something but now recognizes it as a deficit.

Stage 3: Conscious competence: The person now knows how to do something but has to apply complete concentration.

Stage 4: Unconscious competence: The person has developed a personal ritual and can now perform easily and effortlessly with moderate concentration.

Developing **unconscious competence** of the financial habits you will learn in this book will give you a tremendous sense of freedom and joy. It is usually just getting to step one that is the major hurdle for us. Comfort zones are insidious things and need to be challenged regularly. Achieving unconscious competence is not easy, nothing worthwhile ever is, but you'll find that even the process can be exciting and rewarding in and of itself. Before moving on answer these questions concerning your financial habits:

1. How much do you habitually save from every dollar that comes your way?
2. Do you have habits of spending that seem small but actually add up to quite a bit over a week or month?
3. Are you paying for services you don't even use because the amount seems small or it's just too much of a hassle to cancel?
4. What positive financial habit do you want to adopt?

> **"Motivation is what gets you started. Habit is what keeps you going."**
>
> **—Jim Rohn**

Now it is time to listen for...

The Call to Adventure

"The adventure may begin as a mere blunder, as did that of the princess of the fairy tale; or still again, one may be only casually strolling, when some passing phenomenon catches the wandering eye ans lures one away from the frequented paths of man. Examples might be multiplied, ad infinitum, from every corner of the world." (Campbell, The Hero With a Thousand Faces, 1949)

Clues

How will you know if you are being called to your adventure? A life-changing letter that arrives unexpectedly or a white-haired wizard handing you a magical weapon is the stuff of movies. The call will most likely not be quite that obvious. We may not know at first where our call is even coming from or who it is pulling us out of our comfort zone?

Many times the call comes from within us. We have been given a combination of talents and abilities that we share with no other person. We have developed skills and understandings in our lifetime that are unique. The call to adventure beckons to the sleeping hero inside of us to use these attributes. Perhaps some part of us sees a gap, a need that remains unfilled and we just know that we alone are the one uniquely qualified to fill it. This is the part of us that yearns for more and knows we are not living the life we were put here to lead. It calls for us to act on the world in such a way as to leave it better than before.

Define Wealth

If we define exactly what financial independence means for us we will be able to achieve it. Achieving our goal becomes much like navigating a sailboat. If we do not begin with our desired outcome firmly in mind, we have little to focus on out in the horizon. The waves battering our bow easily grab our attention and can lead us off course. The only way to get through the inevitable storms we will face is to set a course beyond where we can see.

Before we talk about financial independence, it is important to define what **wealth** means to us in the first place. Wealth and financial independence are quite different. While they are certainly related concepts, wealth embodies far more than money. I have a definition of wealth that I believe you will agree with.

Wealth: The things that make life worthwhile

You know what these are. They are the health of your loved ones, the laughter and smiles of your friends and children. Wealth is not written on a bank statement. It is not determined by status, salary or net worth. One does not need material riches to be fulfilled, nor does one gain fulfillment from acquiring money. Fulfillment only comes to us through our personal growth and our contribution to others. Wealth and fulfillment are not only attainable but are necessary pursuits for a full and balanced life. Real wealth comes from adding tangible value to the lives of others.

"Help me Obi Wan Kenobi, you're my only hope"

Star Wars

As we have been dramatically reminded of in recent years, wealth does not consist of a specific make of car, the size or location of the house we own or the various other toys adults tend to accumulate. Cars, houses and toys can certainly play a role but they must affirm our purpose, not detract from it. Too often we accumulate things to fill a void in our lives and realize that we have become simply *maintainers of things*. Our time is unequally divided between making a contribution and tending to our warehouse of stuff. Other times we may feel we are being pulled up the status ladder by surrounding ourselves with symbols of wealth instead of pursuing true wealth. Once we identify the things in our life that make it worthwhile, we can rid ourselves of unnecessary hang-ups and faulty concepts of success.

There are many alternative definitions of wealth. In a pure economic sense wealth is relative. It is in comparing ones money or belongings to others that defines a person as wealthy or not. There will always a wealth curve that showcases the **haves** against the **have not's**. Even now during the protracted economic troubles in America, as compared to the rest of the world, there are very few **have not's** among us.

I think we all know deep down that real wealth is not a measurement of us against our neighbor. Pursuing the things that make life worthwhile is really the only accurate definition there is. While it is good to model the actions and behaviors of successful people (in fact mentoring is an essential part of the journey) we must be aware of some of the unrelated beliefs we can pick up from these influences as well. If we choose to define what wealth means to us in advance, we can focus on acquiring only those things that actually enhance our lives and cheerfully omit needless distractions.

What are the things that make your life worthwhile?

What are these things? They are different for everyone. Our aspirations and values are part of what makes us unique. The best way to start is to create a list of the activities, people or things that we feel make it all worthwhile.

Following Bliss

By defining what wealth means to us *on a personal level* we can be prepared to listen for our call to adventure. When we define our purpose we are ready to set goals and begin our journey.

> **"Follow your bliss and the universe will open doors where there were only walls."**
>
> **—Joseph Campbell**

Campbell urges us to find our bliss and follow it not as a suggestion that our work should always be fun but rather as an observation that our psyche will guide us to the life that is waiting for us if we will only take the time and effort to listen.

What does it mean to follow one's bliss? What is bliss anyway?

It might be useful to define bliss by what it is not. Following bliss is not a magical state of problem-free living. It is not that mystical place referred to by some as **Peace of Mind**. These states do not exist except as fleeting moments and lofty ideals. Life is a journey full of challenges, obstacles and problems. The world is full of suffering and sorrow, tragedy and pain. We cannot change this fact but we can instead choose to live with joy despite the sorrows, to say **yes** to life as it is, not as we wish it to be.

Campbell called this the *joyful participation in the sorrows of the world*.

It just might be that it is in the solving of problems for ourselves and for others that we find our bliss. Following bliss is viewing the sum of our talents, skills, interests and desires as a whole. It is listening to our heart. Campbell was vocal in expressing that following bliss is at times antithetical to chasing money. Doing something just for the money often pulls you away from your bliss rather than toward it.

In Bill Moyers's interview, **The Power of Myth**, Campbell said the following:

> **"There's something inside you that knows when you're in the center, that knows when you're on the beam or off the beam, and if you get off the beam to earn money, you've lost your life. And if you stay in the center and don't get any money, you still have your bliss."**

The purpose of your life

> **"Life is without meaning. You bring the meaning to it. The meaning of life is whatever you ascribe it to be. Being alive is the meaning."**

> **Joseph Campbell**

It can be a mistake to fall into the trap of trying to *discover* our purpose, as if it were some mysterious message deeply entrenched in our psyche. While we could spend months or years trying to discover our purpose using complex or arcane methods we can reduce the time involved by simply realizing that our purpose is not something to be discovered but rather what we *define* it to be. Our intuition will guide us to the right answer. We just need to take the right steps to get there.

> **"The simplest explanation for a phenomenon is most likely the correct explanation."**
>
> **—William of Ockham (Ockham's Razor)**

Define Your Purpose

We are all outcome oriented creatures. We tend to thrive on completing tasks and pursuing goals. Our purpose can be thought of as our ultimate outcome. The ultimate reason we do the things we do. When we define our purpose it has the effect of quickening our resolve and helps us more easily identify the things that serve us.

Our purpose is made up of our **values** and our **service to others.**

Our Values

People will make extraordinary efforts to live up to their values. Values are convictions about what is right, good, bad or wrong. They are the limiters of conduct and the ideas that tell us what is worth wanting or expending our energy for.

Our values exist in a hierarchy. This means that some values are more important than others and they are spread along a continuum from most important to least important. The way we describe the importance of one value in relation to another uncovers the metaphor we use internally to store our values. Some people describe closely held values while another would say a value is higher than another. These are simply the mental constructs we have in place to help us keep track of what's important to us.

The important thing to understand is that our values can **and do** change over time or through some extraordinary event in our lives. At these stages, the values may change or just the relative importance of the value.

So how do we determine what are values are? Just ask! Ask yourself the question:

What is most important in my life?

You may come up with answers like **Family** or **Having a Job**. What about family is important? What about having a job is important? Continue to cycle through until the answer no longer leads to another concept. For example, Family could lead to togetherness or love. Togetherness and love are values; Family is a vehicle that helps you meet them. Here is a list of values to get you started.

Creativity, confidence, gratitude, love, respect, playfulness, integrity and achievement are some other examples. Use your own words and write down as many as you can. When you are done choose three that are the most important to you.

Service to Others

What do I want most to do for others? Do I want to teach people to succeed, get fit, a skill? Do I want to inspire, motivate, coach, heal, help, feed or entertain? Find the words that mean the most to you in regards to service to others.

Now arrange your answers in the following format:

My purpose in life is to pursue (**my top 3 values**) while (**my service to others**)

While seemingly simple and formulaic, this method kick starts the process of defining your purpose. Trust your intuition. Take this simple sentence that you constructed and read it aloud. Does it ring true for you? Refine the words until it does. This process should take no longer than an hour if you stick to it. You probably need to get past some false positives before you arrive at a defined purpose that resonates with you. Keep working at it until you are satisfied with the outcome. Anything worthwhile is usually found just past the point you want to give up. Once you have completed this exercise, write down your result.

<u>My Purpose:</u>

My purpose in life is to live with gratitude, love and integrity while teaching others how to become financially independent.

Do what you are and wealth will follow

Often, the seed of our true vocation was planted while we were children. When we were allowed to play we would naturally gravitate toward things that interested us. Over time we find it easy to dismiss these activities as child's play and unimportant. Resist that urge and remember, as vividly as you can the things you wanted most to do as a child. Do you remember who you wanted to be? What you wanted to do when you grew up? It is sometimes within these childhood fantasies that our calling or vocation is found.

Do what you are means simply to identify what your talents, desires and intuition have always communicated to you and to share these gifts with as many people as you can.

Do what you love or do what you are?

It is often said that we need to do what we love in order to be truly happy. In many ways I agree with this, the only problem with it is the lack of a shared definition on the word **love**. The concept of love is often affixed to all sorts of things that are not aligned with our talents and intentions. We love chocolate, sports and baby animals. We love TV, video games and romance novels. Love is blind as the saying goes and chasing after activities we love may lead us away from our true calling.

Focusing on just doing what you love can pull you into the **hobby trap**. It is important to be passionate about what you do but it is equally important to align it with a greater purpose. Passion without purpose is like a gas fire; Lots of heat, flames and smoke with little overall impact. Seth Godin insists that a balance needs to be struck, passion for the task at hand and passion for the overall mission.

> *"It's more important that you be passionate about what you do all day than it is to be passionate about the product that is being sold."*
>
> **—Seth Godin**

How do we do what we are?

The challenge is twofold. Once we discover what we are passionate about we can set goals that will help enable us to pursue these activities. We often dismiss thinking about our passions as being childish or escapist. You might ask yourself the following questions:

"How could I turn something I enjoy into a vocation?"

"If I enjoy it then it's not really work. Isn't that cheating somehow?"

"My parents struggled and worked hard their entire life. Isn't doing work that I enjoy being dishonest?"

The truth of it is that these two things are mutually beneficial. **Hard Work** helps you develop your passion, to bring your ideas into the world. **Passion** pushes you to work hard even after you want to stop because you're tired and want to go home. The harder you work, the more passionate you become. The more passionate you are, the harder you work. What's more, when you are in a state of flow, the hard work you are doing in pursuit of your goals feels effortless, your passion seems to carry you along.

The following questions are designed to help us figure this out. Spend time on these questions. It is within these answers that you may discover your true calling, your vocation. This is the vehicle by which you live the life that you are supposed to live for the benefit of others. It is when we enrich the lives of others in some way, through our vocation and service, that we are rewarded. It is when we follow our own bliss that we are truly able to enrich the lives of others.

If I knew tomorrow would be my last day on earth, that I would be dead by midnight, would I still do what I am about to do?

What would I do instead?

What have I always wanted to accomplish but have never gotten around to?

What did I love to do most when I was a child?

When I was 7, what did I want to be when I grew up?

How can I help others learn, grow and enjoy their lives?

What have my talents, desires and intuition always told me I should do?

What type of work would I do even if I was not paid for it?

Know Your Outcome

Once you have defined your purpose, setting goals becomes easier and more natural. A goal (or an outcome) is simply a result you want. Whether it is a new house, a level of financial abundance, to send your kids to college or to speak a foreign language, our desired outcomes are usually somewhat in line with our values. If we value honesty and integrity, for instance, it is unlikely we would choose a goal that would require violating these. We are outcome seeking creatures by nature and when we make a conscious effort to align our goals to our purpose we start to awaken our sleeping hero.

Milestones are the steps we take to reach our outcomes. A goal can have many milestones along the way or just a few. How many will depend on the complexity of the goal and the **stretch** (the distance between where you are now and where your goal is). If a goal is a specific net worth for example, some milestones might be paying off a debt, opening an investment account, reading a book on the subject investing or putting together a financial independence plan. If you find that there are too many milestones needed to reach your goal, it may be wise to reduce the stretch.

Why Goals?

The purpose of goals and goal setting is not just to "get stuff". If your goals are just about things and money you will get them but you may find that you are still not fulfilled.

> *"The major reason for setting a goal is for what it makes of you to accomplish it. What it makes of you will always be the far greater value than what you get."*
>
> *—Jim Rohn*

The Paradox of Choice

Barry Schwartz, in a 2005 TED talk, rebuked the idea that "*the way to maximize freedom is to maximize choice*". He asserts that too much choice can be overwhelming and lead to mental paralysis. Having a well-defined purpose and positive financial habits will enable you to handle the additional choices with confidence. When you don't have these habits, as is the case with many lottery winners, too much choice can be a curse. We'll add this crucial component to our definition from before since financial independence is as much a state of mind as it is an amount of money:

Financial independence is the diligent conversion of work into passive income and the development of positive financial habits.

Now that we have a good working definition, what does it take to be financially independent?

What's Your FIT?

One way to think of this is with the acronym **F.I.T**. Think of it as being *financially fit*. FIT in this case stands for your ***Financial Independence Threshold*** and is made up of just three numbers that will help you determine what being financially free means *to you*. The components of FIT are your **net worth** *(assets – liabilities)*, your ongoing **monthly expenses** and your **time frame**.

What will it take for you to **feel** financially free? Financial independence, like everything else in our lives, is an emotional state. The amount of money **it costs to be you** is a personal decision based on your lifestyle choices and spending rituals. By creating a realistic, concrete goal around the area of financial independence, you are better able to achieve it.

1. **Net Worth**: How much do you want to have, free and clear? Remember that net worth is all of your stuff *minus* all that you owe.
2. **Expenses**: How much does it cost every month to be you? These are your monthly expenditures.
3. **Time Frame**: How long do you want to have this level of financial independence? 10 years, 5 years, the rest of your life? Perhaps you would just like to work toward taking a sabbatical from your current job.

Having a time frame as part of this definition may seem illogical to some. Isn't financial freedom *forever*? It could be if that is what you choose but don't limit yourself to that criteria just yet. Perhaps a sabbatical is one of your goals. Perhaps a stint of volunteer work in a foreign country is the way you have decided to contribute. Perhaps you want to go back to school and finish that degree, learn something new or train for a new career. What is important is that you define the timeframe of your financial independence goal in order to have a concrete number to reach for. It is a simple equation:

FIT = Net Worth + (Expenses * Time Frame)

Example:

I want to have 3 years of financial freedom in order to pursue x

I anticipate my monthly expenses will be $2,000 ($24,000 per year) for this period. At the end of 3 years, I want to have $24,000 free and clear

$24,000 + $72,000 = $96,000 (your expected expenses over 3 years)

Your FIT in this scenario is $96,000

X might be charity work, volunteering, starting a business, pursuing a dream or even changing careers. Keep in mind that your initial **FIT** will probably change as you learn the wealth habits. For instance, the habit of frugality can reduce your expenses drastically and significantly shorten the amount of time it will take to reach your goal.

A word of caution, do not make *leisure* your FIT goal. You will find that golf, travel, sun and fun wear off rather quickly. A life of leisure is not a healthy part of the human experience. Retirees know this and so does anyone who has taken the opportunity to do so. You must be engaged in your passion and service to others in order to be happy.

Develop your financial independence plan

Many of the tasks we have worked on so far have been to understand, *fully and completely*, where we are financially. Our **net worth** provides a snapshot of how well the habits we currently have are moving us toward financial independence. Our **expenses list** provides a snapshot of what we spend money on regularly and will highlight places where we can make improvements. Our **FIT** gives us a tangible, realistic future target to go for. Knowing where we are is not enough, we must decide where we want to go and why.

Aligning purpose with outcome

Now that we have defined our purpose, which outcomes are we committed to? Write down the answers to the following questions.

> What are the things I want to achieve in my life in 30 years?
> In 10 years?

What goals do I want to reach in the next 6?

What are my desired health outcomes?

What are my desired financial outcomes?

What is my FIT?

How much money have I invested?

What is my income?

What insurance have I obtained?

How much have I reduced my consumer debt?

What do I want to learn? How do I want to grow?

How do I want to improve my health?

What are my faith and spiritual outcomes?

In what ways do I want to improve my Relationships?

What are some things I want to have?

Now, circle the top 5 outcomes that are most closely aligned with your purpose. Write the date you want to achieve this by and a few sentences describing what achieving these outcomes will do for you and your family.

"A goal is a dream with a deadline"

—Napoleon Hill

For each goal, write down what achieving that goal will do for you and your family? Why is this goal good? Sometimes it takes what Jim Rohn calls Nitty-Gritty reasons to get you motivated. In his book, **Seven Strategies for Wealth and Happiness**, he recounts how demoralizing it was to find himself lying to a Girl Scout because he could not spare the two dollars it took to buy a box of cookies.

**"I stared after her for what seemed like a very long time. Finally, I closed the door behind me and, leaning my back to it, cried out, "*I don't want to live like this anymore.*

I've had it with being broke, and I've had it with lying. I'll never be embarrassed again by not having any money in my pocket." **That day I promised myself to earn enough to always have several hundred dollars in my pocket at all times."** (Rohn, The Seven Strategies For Wealth and Happiness)

We need to make sure we have strong reasons to reach our goals. Negative reasons and positive reasons combine to provide a powerful driving force.

Create a plan

For each goal, brainstorm a few milestones that will get you there. Start by writing a detailed description of your goal along with the exact achievement date. Work backwards to today fleshing out the steps necessary to reach the goal. By taking the time to do this process, you will find that you have created the path from where you are to where you want to be. I am a visual person and find it useful to draw an outcome time-line. Get out a big sheet of blank paper and write your outcome in a bubble on the far right and today's date in a bubble on the far left. Start to fill in answers to these questions:

What can I do right now to move me towards this goal?

What is the last thing I need to do before I reach this goal? The next last? (Continue to work backward to today)

Who can help me?

What do I need to learn?

What has to happen before this goal is met?

Setting a goal is good. Setting a date is great. Creating a plan will supercharge the process.

Refusal of the Call

"Often in life, and not infrequently in the myths and popular tales, we encounter the dull case of the call unanswered; for it is always possible to turn the ear to other interests. Refusal of the summons converts the adventure into its negative. Walled in boredom, hard work, or "culture," the subject loses the power of significant affirmative action and becomes a victim to be saved." (Campbell, The Hero With a Thousand Faces, 1949)

The hero of myth initially refuses the call to adventure. Changes of any kind evoke all manner of fears in us all. Uninvited changes in our routine or our lifestyle are usually met with fear or anger (Anger can be thought of as fear turned outward). Even the bravest of warriors hesitates when summoned forth on what he believes to be a perilous journey.

Why Do We Refuse The Call?

We may have beliefs about money, work or service that hold us back. We may be afraid to change what we are used to doing. We are called to adventure from the part within us that knows no limitations. We refuse the call when our fears appear to us bigger than they actually are.

Star Wars Luke Skywalker's response to Obi Wan's request for help "Listen, I can't get involved! I've got work to do! It's not that I like the Empire, I hate it, but there's nothing I

can do about it right now. *It's such a long way from here!"*

It is when we discover who we truly are that we can begin the process of change. Right now there are things you need to do, responsibilities you have and obligations you need to fulfill. You may have a job that barely pays your bills. You may have credit card bills, a car payment or two, medical bills or any other manner of financial burdens. We'll address these specifically when we talk about the five rituals of wealth but for now it is important to know what it is that stops us so we can confidently move forward.

Joseph Campbell, in his study of the myth of the hero, understood the role our refusal of the call plays in our lives.

> *"We must let go of the life we have planned, so as to accept the one that is waiting for us."*
>
> **—Joseph Campbell**

The biggest single factor that makes people refuse their call to adventure seems to be their limiting beliefs about what they are capable of.

What stops me? Am I not strong enough or smart enough? Am I too old or young, too heavy or skinny? Do I have enough education? Taking stock of what stops you will help you determine where you need to shore things up. What is not useful, however, is becoming overwhelmed by what you think you lack. Countless people have started their journey with less money, fewer friends and more problems than you and I. What they had was the courage to begin.

Start where you are.

Your current role is the vehicle that will take you to your true vocation. One of my favorite thoughts on this subject comes from Jim Rohn, he said:

"Work harder on yourself than you do at your job."

—Jim Rohn

You absolutely need to do focus on doing a great job at whatever you are currently laying your hands on. You should always strive to do great work that you can be proud of. What is more important though is that you need to **work harder on yourself**. Work hard on your passion, your true calling. Study hard. Stay up late and get up early. Read books, take courses, spend time with a mentor (more on that in the next chapter). If you are currently unemployed or underemployed you must use your situation as a driving force to discover your passion. When you begin to develop the skills and knowledge that are in line with your talents and desires the **work** part becomes effortless. You are expending energy and time but you find yourself more often in a state of flow.

"Many people give up on learning after they leave school...But a person who forgoes the use of his symbolic skills is never really free. His thinking will be directed by the opinions of his neighbors, by the editorials in the papers, and by the appeals of television."

— Mihaly Csikszentmihalyi Author of Flow

We enter **flow** when we are fully immersed in an activity. When we are doing what we are and our skills become aligned with the challenges before us. There is a balance we need to strike between challenge and skill. Finding flow means developing the habits and skills that will help us meet the challenges we will inevitably face.

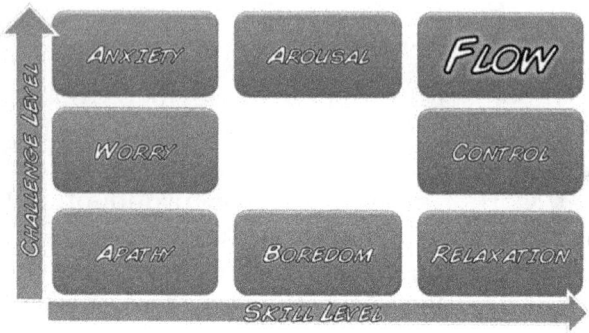

You may be plagued by doubts. How could I make a living doing something I like? What If I am not good enough? No one will pay me to do something I enjoy. It's all a matter of beliefs.

Limiting beliefs

"Why, sometimes I've believed as many as six impossible things before breakfast."

—The White Queen from Lewis Carroll's Through the Looking-Glass

A belief is just the idea that a proposition or a premise is true. It matters little that it **is** true. We mostly just blindly adopt the beliefs of the people around us, never questioning their accuracy. This is how we form a family, a community and a culture. Some beliefs that were useful in the past are no longer useful; perhaps they are even harmful to us. For example, it used to be that finding a good employer and staying with them for our entire working life was the best thing we could do to provide stability for our family. We now know that clinging to that set of beliefs can only bring us disappointment.

Beliefs are extremely powerful as they bring order to our world. What is disconcerting to many is that they are very malleable and changeable. This is disturbing because many beliefs provide the solid ground for us to feel comfortable. It is our convictions about how the world works that brings us the most comfort. Over time your beliefs have changed and evolved.

Changing Minds

Do you believe in Santa? Why not? What changed between when you were a child and now? Beliefs change over time based on new information. You can also change your own beliefs with focused effort.

> *"Common sense is the collection of prejudices acquired by age eighteen." –Albert Einstein*

The first belief we must change is about the nature of **belief** itself. Beliefs are a purely mental construct. No one can argue that Anthony Robbins has not committed the bulk of his life to coach and help others; His philosophy is predicated on the notion that we are the designers of our destiny and we have the power to change our limiting beliefs to ones that empower us. He has come to describe belief as simply a **sense of certainty** that something is true or is not true.

That's it. Sometimes we develop good beliefs from our family and world, other times we don't. Once we understand that we can change our minds, we can begin to **design beliefs** that encourage us.

> *"Beliefs have the power to create and the power to destroy. Human beings have the awesome*

> **ability to take any experience of their lives and create a meaning that disempowers them or one that can literally save their lives."**
>
> **—Anthony Robbins**

Sometimes others put labels on us based on false information. If you now believe that you can learn new skills easily and effortlessly where before you believed you had a learning disability, how much different will your next hour be? Your next day or week? Beliefs are the first mover in your life. Once defined, beliefs guide your behavior throughout the day. Once you create and define beliefs that serve you and discard some of the beliefs that harm you the opportunity to grow increases.

Beliefs That Harm

Let's identify and change some of our doubts (the beliefs that are holding us back). Ask yourself the following questions and write down your answers.

What beliefs do I hold that limit or prevent me from living the life I know I am supposed to live?

What do I believe about the world and our future in general?

What do I believe about the nature of people?

What do I believe about my own ability to become financially independent?

How do others label me?

Beliefs That Serve

Adding a few new beliefs about our capabilities can crowd out doubt.

What are four new beliefs that I would rather have and live with?

What am I really capable of?

What is something I did in the past that I was truly proud of? What did I believe about myself then that made the difference?

What new label do I want to live by?

Self-Talk

Before mobile phones, talking to yourself in public was a sure sign that there was something wrong with you. It turns out that talking to yourself is one of the most powerful ways to change a limiting belief (and now you can get away with it since people will naturally assume you are on the phone). Pick a phrase that is inspiring and embodies your new belief and repeat it to yourself over and over. It could be a statement likes *"I am getting stronger every day"* or a question like *"How did I get so confident and competent?"* If you are nervous about an upcoming speech try *"How did I become such a great communicator?"* If you feel like you can't learn or adapt to change easily try something like *"I can learn new things quickly and easily"*. Choose words that fit. Focus on capabilities rather than tangibles. What do I mean by this? Avoid saying "*I am Rich*" but rather say "*I am developing powerful money habits*". Building a belief about a general capability is much more powerful than one that focuses on a particular skill.

Self-talk is referred to also as affirmations or incantations. I prefer the term *self-talk* since it is not loaded with a bunch of weirdness. The word *affirmation* brings to me an image of Stuart Smalley:

"I'm good enough, I'm smart enough, and dog-gone it, people like me"

—Al Franken as Stuart Smalley on SNL

There is nothing mystical or fantastic going on here. By repeating a positive phrase over and over, it simply crowds out negativity and instills a new, self-fulfilling belief in its place. After a while, you start to **believe** the concepts that were before just strings of words. Talk to yourself in this way when you are jogging, driving or doing chores. We have become so accustomed to always being entertained that we forget to control the influences coming our way. It may sound a bit hyperbolic but try this for 30 days and I am certain that this one habit will open up all sorts of new possibilities for you.

We are bombarded each day by negative messages from print, television, the internet and by extension our friends and family (who are influenced by the same pool of information). The economy, the next election and foreign affairs are almost always negatively portrayed in the news. **"If it bleeds, it leads"** is the 24/7 news cycle mantra. It is good to be informed about what is going on but be careful not to let the medium become the message. When you allow your focus to be only on all that is wrong with people and the world, it is hard not to feel overwhelmed and uncertain. Develop the habit of turning off the negative flow to your brain. Turn off the news, the petty reality show and put down the bitter tabloid. Go for a walk and repeat your new belief.

It is now time for our...

Meeting with the Mentor

 *"...the first encounter of the hero-journey is with a protective figure (often a little old crone or old man) who provides the adventurer with amulets against the dragon forces he is about to pass."* (Campbell, The Hero With a Thousand Faces, 1949)

The mentor of myth was often an elderly figure who gave our hero a special weapon or amulet. He would also accompany him through difficult passages and aid him with kernels of wisdom. The wizard would show up at just the right moment to help the hero make a life altering decision. The Hermit would appear from the forest and protect the hero from certain doom.

Mentors are everywhere. While seldom as dramatic as a space opera or ancient Greek myth, finding the right mentor can be a wonderful experience. Once you know what endeavor your talents, desires and skills point to you can find others who have gone before you. Many times the success they attained was on the backs of failures and mistakes that they can share with you and possibly spare you from some of them. In any activity worth doing you are going to make mistakes. It makes sense to learn as much as you can from the trials of others instead of reinventing the wheel.

Star Wars: "A more elegant weapon from a more civilized age."

—Obi-Wan as he hands Luke
his Fathers lightsaber

Once we have begun to discover and determine our unique gift, it is time to learn how to serve others with it. Whether through art or business or through teaching, coaching or building things, when we align our purpose and vocation, the desire to serve others with our unique gifts become a driving force in our lives.

A Mentor is a person who has gone before us, who has a battle worn shield full of dents and scratches but also a quiver of sharp arrows and a bag full of gold. They are the generation that brought society forward for us to prevail. They are knowledgeable in ways we cannot even imagine. A well-chosen mentor will guide you past the obstacles that hinder and through to the reward that awaits.

It is evidenced again and again that modeling the actions of a successful person is the fastest, surest way to become competent in any endeavor. This is the concept at the core of apprenticeship.

There are a few practical ways to find a mentor in your chosen vocation. Seek out a mentor in your area of interest. Find someone who has succeeded in your calling. Whether it is someone in your current occupation or an advisor from SCORE (Counselors to Americas Small Business- www.score.org), find a mentor and learn from him or her.

Model their successes, learn from their failures. When seeking the counsel of a mentor, don't be afraid to ask about the time they messed up. They could be forthcoming and help you avoid common mistakes in your industry. Immerse yourself in the vocation you have chosen. Get the top three books, videos or courses about your subject and carve out the time to become an expert.

Don't be shy. If you find a mentor that seems out of reach. There is no harm in asking and many times, even if they cannot spare the time they can point you in the right direction. Aim high.

We are now prepared to meet the...

Threshold Guardians

"With the personifications of his destiny to guide and aid him, the hero goes forward in his adventure until he comes to the "threshold guardian" at the entrance to the zone of magnified power. Such custodians bound the world in the four directions – also up and down – standing for the limits of the hero's present sphere, or life horizon. Beyond them is darkness, the unknown, and danger" (Campbell, The Hero With a Thousand Faces, 1949)

> **"Those that say it can't be done should get out of the way of those who are doing it"**
>
> **—Chinese Proverb**

Do what you are means to identify what your talents, desires and intuition have always communicated to you and to find ways to share these gifts with as many people as you possibly can. Only by doing what we are can we truly change our life and the lives of others. By providing value to others, we enrich ourselves; it is a fortuitous cycle that constantly builds momentum. Crossing the threshold from our ordinary world into the world of doing what we are brings out resistance from many areas of our life. We resist ourselves internally. Family, friends and foes may resist us externally. Our personal changes will undoubtedly send out waves that will affect the lives of everyone around us. Change of any kind is disruptive and is often met with fear and suspicion.

Guardians at the Gate

There are internal and external forces that want to keep us where we are. Homeostasis in our body seeks balance. Peer pressure and social norms tend to have a broad, silent hold on our activities. Vindictive or envious people may be more vocal in their discontent. These are our **threshold guardians**. They act in a way that prevents us from becoming who we know we should become. We have already worked on changing some of our limiting beliefs, now we will learn some specific traits and actions that will move us past these guardians and toward our goals.

Fail Forward

In order to grow and learn from our own experiences or that of a mentor, we must understand what failure is. Failure is part of life; in fact, **failure is one of the great keys to success**. Failure is the only place where learning and growth truly happen. Whenever we attempt a new activity, we make mistakes. When we adjust our actions we learn. Learning, at its core, is our persistent and unwavering cognitive response to the mistakes we make. This is true with learning to read, learning a sport or learning a complex skill. Whenever we turn our focus to something new, there are mistakes and failures waiting for us. These are an essential part of learning

Fear of Ridicule

Sometimes we don't dare to act because of the fear of criticism. We don't sing, draw, dance or write. We don't assert our individuality for fear that it will generate a laugh. We allow even the remote threat that we will be ridiculed to lock us down and prevent us from even trying.

When we first try something we are going to bad at it. Many times the myth of natural talent is simply a dedicated person who was willing to fail thousands of times in pursuit of his craft. Too often, because of the fear of being made fun of, we shy away from the risk of a new activity. Instead we prefer the comfort of something we have shown proficiency in, something we are good at. Over time this avoidance tends to narrow our choices and we limit ourselves to comfortable activities.

> **"It is in the character of very few men to honor without envy a friend who has prospered"**
>
> **—Aeschylus**

We must seek out new places to fail. There are things we need to learn how to do. Many times we don't fear failure but the chemical byproduct of failure: Embarrassment. The fear of someone seeing us fail keeps us from even trying. Don't let the fear of embarrassment act like guardrails that keep you confined to a narrow road. Life is way too short to live within the confines of other people's opinions. By embracing failure as simply a stepping stone on the path toward our outcomes we can focus on our personal talents, gifts and skills.

We must learn to look at our mistakes and the mistakes of others not as things to be ridiculed but as essential parts of the experience.

Ironically, the best place to start is with us. Instead of laughing at others mistakes try to be empathetic towards them. By showing true empathy to others when **they** falter, we eliminate our own fears; **compassion**, thrown outward, returns a hundred-fold.

> **"A life spent making mistakes is not only more honorable but more useful than a life spent in doing nothing."**
>
> **—George Bernard Shaw**

We must break through the artificial boundaries that hold us back and identify the obstacles we need to overcome. Obstacles present themselves to us in various ways, some are external and some are within us.

SWOT

At its core, a threshold is made up of both positive and negative attributes. In our quest to achieve any objective there are things that stand in our way and things that help us move forward. These helpful and harmful attributes come from within us or are external in origin. An extremely useful tool that will help you identify both allies and enemies is the SWOT analysis. **SWOT** stands for **Strength, Weakness, Opportunity** and **Threat**. Grab a blank sheet of paper and divide it into 4 equal squares. Label the top two boxes **Strength & Weakness**. Label the bottom two **Opportunity & Threat**. Strengths and weaknesses are internal factors, things you personally bring to the table. Opportunities and threats are things that are part of your environment.

SWOT is a powerful tool to help you understand the things that you already bring to bear on your quest for financial freedom as well as the obstacles you may find in your way. Fill in each square with the answers to the following questions.

Internal Factors

Strengths

What are my strengths?
What am I good at?
Who are my allies?

Weaknesses

What am I bad at?
What do I hate doing?

External Factors

Opportunities

What can help me improve?
Who can I connect with to help me?

Threats

Who are my enemies?
What prevents me from succeeding?
What holds me back?

What will it cost me if I fail to act?

What are the obstacles in my path?

How do I overcome each one?

Who are my threshold guardians?

What right or qualification do they have to advise me?

What right do they have to hold me back?

What are they gaining in their lives by preventing my achievement?

How can I move past these limitations?

Just identifying the threshold guardians in our quest is often enough to embolden us. The road to financial independence requires us to face fear that many times manifests itself as self-doubt, feelings of unworthiness, and even fear of the success we want to attain.

Now that we have identified and know how to defeat our threshold guardians, it's time to adopt...

The Five Rituals of Wealth

> *"I wouldn't worry about money...No, it has a lot to do with happiness, I just meant YOU shouldn't worry, cause you'd just piss it away."*
>
> **—Justin Halpern**
> *(@shitmydadsays via Twitter)*

What is the most important factor that determines if a person becomes financially independent? Is it the amount of money he or she earns? Is it their upbringing or college degrees? Is it testosterone or Karma that determines this type of outcome? Theories abound based on these and many other false assumptions. The simple truth is that it is your financial philosophy and more importantly, your financial **habits** that make 80% of the difference. Earning more and having advanced degrees make less of an impact than many would like to admit. As we see over and over again, even starting out with a large amount of money is no guarantee that you'll keep it.

> **"If someone gives you a million dollars you better become a millionaire quickly so you can keep the money."**

Regardless of your education or vocation there are certain habits that will lead to financial independence. The surest way to wealth is to provide value to others in a manner consistent with your own values. Your relationships, health, knowledge and lifestyle also make up our wealth. Do you remember our definition of wealth?

Wealth: The things that make life worthwhile.

To this we'll add:

The way you handle your money reveals more about your true values than almost anything else.

Money is simply a measure of value. Money is neither good nor evil. Money is not a weapon or a medicine but can be used to purchase both. The first step is to truly understand that we already have the capacity for wealth and fulfillment; in fact we are already wealthy in many ways.

As we discussed, the amount you earn does not matter *that* much, it is the habits you establish around money that matter most. In fact, it seems that a major impediment to wealth building can be obtaining too much money too soon! We have all heard stories of lottery winners and heirs of the rich losing their fortunes. Many of these unfortunate souls are much worse off after receiving this boon than before. How could that be? The habits you have around frugality, investing, ownership, entertainment and contribution are what really matter in the wealth equation. Once you understand this and the other simple rituals, you will understand that not only is it inevitable and predictable, the negative outcome is completely avoidable as well. With these habits established, any amount of money you earn becomes seed capital for a wealthy future. Without these habits, no amount of money can make you financially independent. The most important wealth tools you have are the habits you consistently reinforce.

Regardless of where you are, what stage of life you are in. Whether you are young or old, come from privileged beginnings or poverty, you have the ability to start on your own hero's journey.

Start where you are and start now.

Take Stock

Wealth is made up of the things that make your life worthwhile. Friendships, health, family bonds, pets and appreciation for nature are all examples. Take stock of some of the ways you are already wealthy.

In what ways am I already wealthy?

Health wealth: Am I alive? Am I healthy?

Family wealth: Who do I love? Who loves me?

Financial wealth: Do I have **any** money?

Friendship wealth: Who do I call my friends?

Spiritual wealth: Am I in good standing with my creator? In what ways am I happy to be alive?

It is important that you realize that you are not starting from zero (even if your balance sheet says so). You are already wealthy in many areas. Just being healthy and alive is an enormous source of wealth. The fact that you are able to read this now is a gift.

Rewards

Developing any new ritual that is worthwhile requires discipline. One of the ways to accelerate this process is to set up a system of rewards. Rewards work by giving you instant, pleasurable feelings that work to reinforce behaviors. While you are learning about each of the wealth habits, think of an appropriate reward for yourself. Giving yourself rewards associates pleasure to your actions. These feelings will further drive you to perform until you develop a positive habit at a deep level.

Here are a few great ideas to maximize the effectiveness of your personal rewards. Rewards should be simple, personal and defined in advance. A toy, new dress, a gadget you want (but do not necessarily need) are all good candidates. What is most important is that the reward is personal and relevant. Sometimes giving yourself a free block of time to relax can be the best reward. When you perform your habit once, **reward**. Reward yourself early and often and continue to reward yourself at random intervals over time. Catch yourself doing something right and take a few moments to pat yourself on the back. By associating good feelings to your new habits, you will adopt them faster and ultimately make them stronger. Come up with 10 things that you enjoy that can be used as rewards to reinforce my new wealth habits?

Could these rituals really make me financially free? Absolutely! Millionaires in our society tend to share a common set of values. They value thrift, discipline, economic achievement and financial independence. There are habits that encourage these values and habits that defy them. There are five habits or rituals that, if adopted, will undoubtedly lead to wealth.

The five wealth rituals will make you financially independent, they have for many people who have chosen to adopt them. SO, what are the five rituals?

Wealth Ritual One: **Pay Your Wealth First**

Wealth Ritual Two: **Be Frugal**

Wealth Ritual Three: **Be Your Own Boss**

Wealth Ritual Four: **Cover Your Assets**

Wealth Ritual Five: **Live with an Attitude of Gratitude**

Let's start our wealth building journey with...

Wealth Ritual One: Pay Your Wealth First

Once you begin earning money you quickly realize that there are lots of people wanting a slice of your financial pie. Your rent, car payment, electric bill, food and phone can suck out most of it. Tickets, date night, a movie and diapers can suck out the rest. Once you are done paying your obligations and having a little fun there is not much left for long term wealth building. That is precisely why this habit makes so much sense. It is a psychological trick that really works. Instead of building wealth with what's left, we **build the foundation of our financial independence first** and then live on what's left. **Simple shift, huge difference.**

Decide right now to pay your wealth the first dime out of every dollar you receive and you will become financially independent. It works. You learn in very short order that living on what's left after your wealth investment is easy, effortless. You just do not miss it.

Several excellent books on money and investing call this principle **pay yourself first**. This is great advice if understood in the proper context. We are all complex people. Our *self* is made up of many facets just like the surface of a diamond. The richness of our personality is sometimes found in the internal conflicts that we have and how we resolve them. **Pay your wealth first** means to invest first in that part of your **self** that desires long term financial independence not in the part of you that wants short term pleasures.

Dimes

Paying your wealth first is deciding in advance what to do with all of the money that flows through your life. You can think of this strategy simply as **dimes out of every dollar**. Establishing the habit of **investing** the first dime out of every dollar that comes in will lead you to financial independence. It has for many thousands of people. This habit is very easy to establish. In fact, with direct deposit and automatic bank transfers it is easier now than ever before. You could set it once and forget it.

Let's look at an example:

Imagine that you decide to have 10% of your pay automatically invested every pay period.

If you are 25 and earn exactly $35,000 per year for 40 years, over 1.4 million dollars will pass through your hands by the time you reach retirement age. If you pay your wealth just the first dime out of every dollar, you will have over 1 million dollars at age 67. This is assuming that you **never get a raise** and you get an 8% rate of return on your investments. An 8% rate of return is an achievable outcome and with a long enough time horizon, it could be considerably more. Paying your wealth first is hard at first. It requires commitment, tenacity and strength but it can be done.

Let's look at two more examples:

If you start at age 50 earning $75,000 per year and pay yourself 10% you will still have a respectable **$220,000** in just 15 years. Not too bad. It is never too late to begin this amazing habit.

If you start at age 25 earning $40,000 per year and pay yourself 10% you will have a **half a million dollars** before your reach your 55th birthday.

But what if you are starting at age 23 earning just $20,000 per year? It might be hard to believe but 1.7 million dollars will pass through your hands over the course of your earning lifetime. If you pay yourself the first dime from every dollar you'll still have over **1 million dollars** in investments.

These numbers don't include the value of your home or any other assets, just the future value of a dime from every dollar. It is also unlikely that your income will stay the same over the course of your lifetime. Chances are it will rise in lockstep with inflation. Is financial independence worth $10.00 a day?

How much do you really have to earn to earn a dollar? It's not 100 cents. Most people have to earn about $1.30 to earn a dollar. This depends on your tax rate. It is important to only count your money after it has passed through the filter of taxes. All of the wealth rituals you'll learn have an additional effect of reducing your taxable income. By developing **The Five Rituals of Wealth**, you also take advantage of tax savings related to owning your own business, owning your own home, investing in tax deferred/tax free vehicles and even giving generously to the charity of your choice.

Start where you are.

This habit, like all others begin with meaning. What is the meaning you personally assign to saving money? To investing? Go for the personal answers, not the Oxford Dictionary ones.

What does saving money mean to me?

What does investing mean to me?

If you are not paying your wealth first by saving or investing, the meaning you have about these concepts is probably at fault. If saving means *sacrifice* or *going without* you are unlikely to engage in it even with the possibility of future millions. If investing means *risk*, *loss* or *too complicated* you probably won't do that either.

One of the major beliefs that prevent people from forming the ten-percent habit is the Richest Man in the Graveyard fallacy.

"Why should I scrimp and go without just so I can be an old person with a bunch of money. I'll be too old to enjoy it"

Forming this habit is not sacrifice, its **liberation**. The feelings you get by knowing you are on the path to financial independence will permeate other areas of your life. Well before you reach retirement age you will gain the enormous benefit if this wealthy habit. You will quickly realize how valuable this lifestyle and financial philosophy really is. This is not about getting rich *someday.* It is about *living wealthily every day*.

Pay your wealth first means freedom. It means investing in your own security and joy. When you pay your wealth first, you are asserting your discipline in ways that will bring you far more than financial abundance.

Don't get hung up on rates of return or anything else. Fear of making an investment mistake just stops you from taking action. *The purpose here is to start where you are and establish a habit*. Put the money in a credit union account. If you feel you cannot trust yourself not to binge on this money while you are forming this habit, open an account at a bank 100 miles away. Make it easy to deposit but difficult to withdraw. Most banks give out a check card for use at an ATM. Don't get one with this account. It must be a one-way street. Money goes in, nothing comes out. Put a note on your calendar to put 10% of everything you earn into this account every time you get paid or set up an automatic transfer.

The Second Dime

The second dime out of every dollar is used to eliminate consumer debt.

Debt is the slavery of the free.

Consumer debt is self-imposed slavery. You are trading your future labor and effort for short term gain. You must stop incurring new debt and pay off the debt you already have.

It might seem like a better plan to pay off debt first and then start saving. From a purely logical point of view it makes sense. If you are heavily in debt you are probably paying significant amounts of interest on these loans so paying off debt first seems like the rational way to go. One challenge with this approach is that *our relationship with money is emotional, not logical.* It is our habits and rituals as well as the meanings we have about spending and investing that drive our behavior. When we simultaneously invest and pay down our debts we are establishing two very powerful and life changing habits at the same time. These habits continually reinforce each other and as our debt is paid off more money becomes available for wealth building.

It is important to understand why people get into debt in the first place. It usually starts off innocently enough. A credit card in college or new car loans are examples of this. Spending *money we don't have* on *things we don't need* puts us firmly on the road to financial hardship. Corporations want us to buy their stuff and banks want to lend us money to do so. Even leaders in our government argue that the primary way to bolster the economy is through consumer lending. Let's be clear though, *it is not patriotic to be poor.* You will do far more good for our great society by being a good steward of your money.

When you pay your wealth first and eliminate debt **at the same time** you simultaneously develop two powerful habits.

The Third Dime

The third dime from every dollar is to be given to charity.

How we treat the less fortunate among us is our true test of character. We have a deep need to contribute. Giving to the charity of your choice is great for the recipients and great for you. There are several excellent reasons to give. The most important reason to give is to help others. A secondary but less often cited reason to give is that people who give tend to approach life with a sense of opportunity and abundance. In a recent study of millionaires, it was implied that their habits of charity actually allowed them to see opportunity where others did not. The Social Capital Community Benchmark Survey (SCCBS) was conducted a few years ago and had some interesting results. More giving doesn't just correlate with higher income; it seems to **cause** higher income. In a simple sense, giving and volunteering make people happy. In the survey, people who gave money to charity were 43% more likely to say that they were "Very Happy". (Harvard University, 2000)

Giving money, giving blood and volunteering make people much happier and will significantly reduce their levels of stress. People who are happy and less stressed are more productive. Creativity flows when you are happy and relaxed. Conversely, being stressed and sad tends to lock you down. Regardless of the personal rewards giving brings you, helping people who need it is just the right thing to do.

Charity Challenge

Try an experiment. Give money to a charity every day for the next 10 days. It does not have to be much but more than you normally would give. Choose a charity or charities that feel strongly about. The decision of what organization to give to is highly personal. Think about where you would like your contribution to make an impact. Rate your happiness and sadness on a scale from 1 to 10 before the experiment and again afterwards. I am 100% certain that you will be amazed by this.

> *"You can give without loving, but you cannot love without giving."*
>
> **—Amy Carmichael**

Find Your Plan

Here are the ideal numbers for you to go for.

10% pay your wealth

10% debt elimination

10% charity

70% is what you live on.

What's Your Zero?

Before starting on this journey my **zero** was **zero**. That is, only when my bank balance reached $0.00 did I admit I was out of money. When you are first starting out it is critical that you build a cash cushion. Before you start investing heavily in a retirement fund, the stock market or any other investment vehicle, you need to establish a contingency fund. Job loss, health problems or other unplanned financial events can arrive at any time. Having a contingency fund protects you and your family from these events. It is a buffer from the unexpected. Your contingency fund should be equal to at least 6 months of living expenses. Decide what that is for you. This amount usually does not need to completely replace your income but should be ample enough to get you back on your feet and into the game. This is your *Zero*!

It is interesting that as you eliminate debt and develop frugal habits, the actual amount you need in this fund goes down. The **cost of being you** has dropped and so has the need for a larger cash cushion.

One exception is that if you are heavily in debt you could start with a 5—20—5 plan (5% pay yourself, 20% Debt payment, 5% charity) and pay down the loans that are charging the most interest.

Adjust the percentages but not the habits.

Once you eliminate your consumer debt, increase your pay your wealth contribution to 20%.

Vehicles and Buckets

In the early stages of your plan there aren't many decisions to make about where your investments should go. The best choice for your contingency fund is in a money market account at a credit union or in an FDIC insured bank account. It does not earn much, if any, interest but the goal of this money is to be there if you need it. Zero risk of loss is the name of this game.

Once you have eliminated debt and have funded 6 months of your contingency fund deciding on the right **investment vehicle** can be daunting. There are so many things to choose from.

You can think of this process as a series of buckets stacked on top of each other. As the top bucket fills the overflow cascades over to the next bucket until all of them are full. In this scenario each bucket represents a specific investment vehicle.

Buckets

I have set up an example of someone who works at a company that offers a 401(k). If you are self-employed you can use a solo 401(k) or defined benefit plan and the numbers work out just about the same. It is a hierarchy of importance. After you take care of necessities and pick the low hanging fruit you move on to accelerating your drive to financial independence.

1. **Contingency Fund**: The first bucket to fill is your contingency fund. This is 6 months'

worth of income replacement. The purpose is to provide a buffer from unforeseen financial setbacks and to help get yourself back on your feet. While you are funding this, you must *eliminate* any consumer debt you have.

2. **Free Money Match**: The second bucket may not be available to everyone but is worth describing. Some employers will give you matching dollars up to a certain percentage of your 401(k) retirement plan contribution. **This is free money** and you should invest at least up to the match threshold. If your company matches 3%, then definitely invest 3%. It has the added effect of possibly reducing your taxes as well.

3. **Tax Advantaged *Long Term* Investments**: Open an IRA account. I recommend opening one at either Vanguard or T. Rowe Price. $5,000 is the maximum you can contribute to a Traditional IRA or Roth IRA. You can mix and match the two as long as the total contribution is under the limit. I recommend the Roth IRA for most people. It is funded with after tax earnings but provides more flexibility than a Traditional IRA. Vanguard.com has an excellent comparison of the two. If you can't decide which one to open, call T. Rowe Price and open both, set up automatic bank transfers so that your Roth and Traditional IRA reaches $2500 each by December 31st. That comes to $208 per month per IRA ($416 total per month). *If this is all you do you will have close to $220,000 accumulated after 20 years* (assuming a very attainable 7% return)

4. **Max out your 401(k)**: $16,500 per year is the current 401(k) maximum. What is

great is that the employer match from bucket 2 does not count against this total.

Is this Dollar Cost Averaging?

You may have heard about dollar cost averaging as an investment tool. **Dollar Cost Averaging** is investing a fixed amount of money at fixed intervals of time. Our monthly investment schedule has us investing into mutual funds on the same day each month. It is easy and automatic. Some months the stock or bond fund will have a low price and you will get more units, other months it will be trading higher and you will get less. Studies suggest that over time this fluctuation will help you get a better return than if you had invested a lump sum all at once.

What Investments Should I Choose?

Famously, Ben Graham, author of **The Intelligent Investor** which is perhaps the most influential investment book of all time said in his 1934 book, **Security Analysis**:

"An investment operation is one which, upon thorough analysis, promises safety of principal and a satisfactory return. Operations not meeting these requirements are speculative."

Speculation is another word for gambling. It should be noted that Warren Buffet attributes much of his success to Ben Graham's teachings and philosophy. The flip side of speculative investing is **value investing**. The essence of value investing is buying stocks at less than their intrinsic value. The difficult part is determining what a company's **intrinsic value** really is. This takes focus, hard work and dedication plus a *smattering* of good luck. If you have determined that value investing is your bliss and you are willing to invest 100% into the endeavor then go for it. Read **The Intelligent Investor** and all of

Berkshire Hathaway's annual reports and you'll be off to a good start. For all others (including myself) just invest in the whole market.

Whatever your situation, you should invest in a broad—based stock index fund and a broad bond index fund. The split should be based on your age. John Bogle says that **bonds equal to your age** are an excellent split. For example, a 25 year old puts 75% into a stock fund and **his age**, 25%, into a bond fund. Easy peasy.

Asset Allocation

Asset Allocation is simply how much of your investment pie gets placed into different investments. The major investment types are stocks, bonds and cash. You can think of your contingency fund as your investment in cash so what's left is your stock/bond split. In our example scenario we have decided upon a 70/20/10 split. 70% are stocks, 20% bonds and 10% cash (or cash equivalent). While it has the effect of reducing the potential long term gain, having at least 10% of your assets in cash is an important psychological cushion.

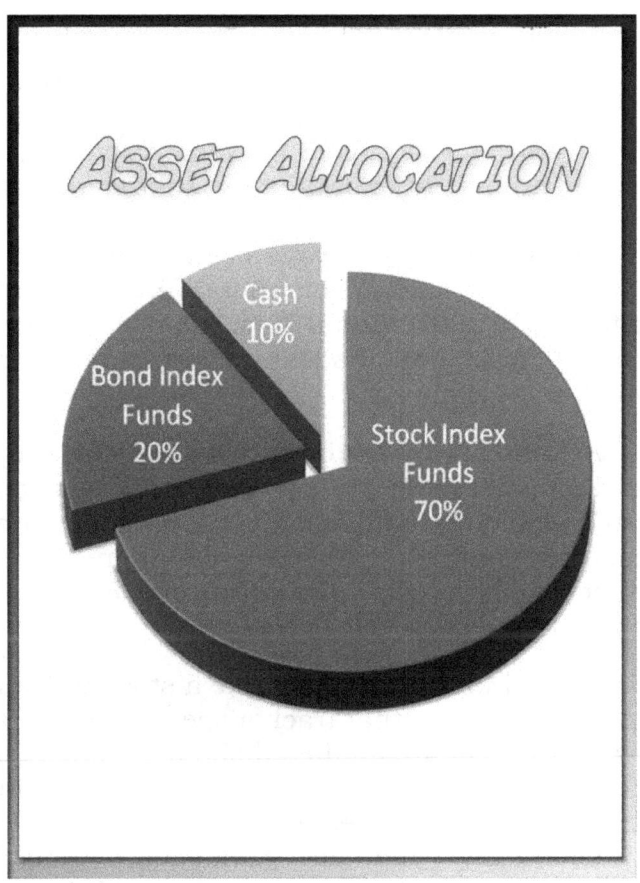

Stocks vs. Bonds...fight!

Which is better, stocks or bonds? I think you'll find that both are necessary for a smart and balanced portfolio.

A Stock is a part ownership of a company. In exchange for a few dollars, you get a **share** of the company. A company can pay you a bit of its profit (*a dividend*) every once in a while or keep that money with the promise that the value of the stock will grow. If you put $1 in the stock market in 1929 you would be...very old today. You may have heard examples like this which tout great promise if you could go back in time and make decisions like this. It is important to note that stocks are a necessary part of your investment portfolio but unfortunately; many of the statistics used in determining the effectiveness of stock investing rely on unrealistic scenarios. Stocks can drop, and stay dropped, for **long** stretches. This is something the "*stocks return an average of 9% over the past 100 years*" people don't readily own up to. Stocks have always been volatile and are even more so today. You should invest a portion into stock index funds but balance them with bonds. When we discuss rebalancing, I think you'll completely agree.

A Bond is an **I.O.U.** You loan a company or government some money **now** in exchange for more money **later**. Instead of paying a credit card company interest, you get paid interest by the issuer of the bond. What a concept! Be a lender, not a borrower.

A bond index fund, just like a stock index fun, is a bag of bonds that track a specific index. Bond index funds are quite different things than holding individual bonds. They track an index and offer you far greater flexibility. Bond funds automatically reinvest dividends, individual bonds do not. If you invested $10,000 in the Vanguard Long Term Bond Index Fund in 2001, you would have over $21,000 today; a 10 year return of 7.93% on a very stable, reliable investment.

By allocating a percentage to bonds and a percentage to stocks and periodically making adjustments to keep the percentages the same, you overcome the weaknesses in both stocks and bonds. (More on this in a minute when we discuss *rebalancing*)

Own The Entire World!

Wouldn't it feel good to own the whole world? Well, you can and it happens to be the investment strategy advocated by such personal finance big leaguers as Andrew Tobias (author of

The Only Investment Guide You'll Ever Need), Burton Malkiel and Charles Ellis (*The Elements of Investing*) and John Bogle (Bestselling author of numerous financial books, inventor of the *index* mutual fund and founder of the Vanguard Group). Investing your hard earned money in a few **broad-based index mutual funds** is the best way to become financially independent.

Broad-Based

A stock mutual fund is just a bag of stocks. It could be a bag holding the stocks of energy companies, big multi-national corporations or small, up and coming businesses. To own a broad-based mutual fund means to own a small piece of hundreds of companies, both large and small, from around the world. An example is the *Vanguard Total World Stock Index Fund (VTWSX)*. This fund holds in its bag, stocks from companies all over the world. This is one way, to paraphrase Andrew Tobias, for the **small investor to share in the growth of the world economy**. Broad based is just another way of saying *diversified*. By spreading out the risk your potential loss, if any of the companies in the bag fails, is greatly reduced.

Robot Management

There are two types of mutual funds. Actively managed and indexed. An index is sort of a benchmark or temperature gauge that is used to measure the health of the particular market or even the health of the overall economy. The Dow Jones Industrial Average (DJIA) and the Standard and Poor's 500 (S&P 500) are the most commonly cited ones in the news but there are many more. An *index fund*, whether stock or bond, owns the same assets that are represented by the *index* it tracks.

Origins: Back in 1896, Charles Dow added up the prices

of the 12 biggest companies in the U.S. and divided that number by 12. The first Stock Index was born. It was simple math for a simpler time. Now there are several major indices with varying levels of computational complexity.

Man in the Middle

An Actively managed fund has a heartbeat attached to it. There is a person (or *persons*) who actively go out and buy and sell stocks or bonds to be included in the mutual fund. These people wear expensive suits and drive very nice cars. Index funds, on the other hand, employ robots who simply track an index. When the index, like the S&P 500, adds or drops a stock, the index fund robot does the same thing. Since this is a relatively rare occurrence, transaction fees are lower and the robot gets plenty of downtime.

How important are expenses?

The expense ratio is the fee that the mutual fund charges you to own it. This cost is represented by a percentage. In general, index funds, *since robots are not very demanding* (yet!), have much lower expenses than actively managed funds. Even half a point (0.5%) can have a huge impact on your overall returns. Vanguard and T. Rowe Price have a strong reputation for providing high levels of quality service with very low expense ratios. If the robots become self-aware and start wearing Armani suits then this could all change...for the worse.

Rebalancing Act

Over time your asset allocation will drift out of whack. Perhaps the stock market will soar driving the relative value of your stock index fund higher so that your 60%/40% stock/bond split that you intended is now at 80%/20%. What should you do? Investing wisdom suggests that your stock funds may be **overvalued** and your bond funds may be **undervalued**. In this case you would sell off some of your stock fund holdings and buy some bond shares to bring your asset allocation back to your target. Using the 70/20/10 Asset Allocation from before, this is what might see if stocks drop and bonds rise. In this case, sell your bond holdings and buy stock funds. The NAV (Net Asset Value or trading price) of the stock index funds will have gone down so you will be able to purchase many more of them. You are selling high and buying low, the holy grail of investing!

REBALANCE: SELL 20% OF BONDS & BUY STOCKS

Cash 10%

Bond Index Funds 40% TARGET 20%

Stock Index Funds 50% TARGET 70%

SCENARIO:
BOND FUND PRICE INCREASED 20%,
STOCK FUND PRICE DOWN 20%

Conversely, if the stock market crashes and for argument's sake your stock portion is 20% and your bond portion is 80% (extreme example!) you should first panic (everyone is entitled to a bit of panic) and then **pull it together** and take advantage of the bargain presented to you. Or, in the sage words of the world's greatest investor:

> **"Be fearful when others are greedy and be greedy when others are fearful."**
>
> **—Warren Buffet**

Sell your bonds and buy stock index fund shares at rock-bottom prices. The jury is still out on how often you should rebalance your accounts in order to bring them back into your target asset allocation. Some say every 6 months while others recommend once every year. I like to rebalance every 6 months and additionally if there is a significant financial event like the ones we discussed that causes the accounts to go 15% or more out of balance. The drawback to frequent rebalancing is that it incurs additional management fees that will eat up your returns.

Target Retirement Funds

One way to shortcut all of this is just to choose a target retirement fund to invest in. These funds determine the **asset allocation** and **rebalancing frequency** based on your age or how long you have until you plan on retiring. You give up a little control but gain a stable, low stress investment. An excellent example is the Vanguard target retirement fund portfolio. Depending on your age, they invest in the Vanguard Total Stock Market Index, International Stock Index and the Total Bond Market funds. While most of Vanguard's funds have a minimum investment of $3,000, the target funds can be started with only a $1,000 minimum investment and charges a very low 0.18% expense ratio. You can then set up an automatic monthly transfer from your bank. **Set it and forget it!**

It is important to reiterate that you should continue to eliminate your debt **while** you are investing. Adjust the percentages but always do your investments and debt elimination in parallel. Again, this may seem counterintuitive especially if you are paying high interest on credit card debt and only earning 0.2% in a checking account. This imbalance will be corrected over time; it is the **habit** that is most important.

But what about options, IPOs, puts, calls, etc...

As you'll learn later on, the financial media is an enemy to your wealth and should be avoided. Stockbrokers, pundits and all types of financial gurus are eager to separate you from your money. You can't beat the market. Owning a broad-based portfolio of stock index funds and bond index funds is the best way to invest.

Summary

Start where you are:

10% — Pay your wealth

10% — Eliminate Debt

10% — Give to charity

70% — Live your life

If you have high consumer debt, adjust these percentages accordingly but do not eliminate a category entirely. Regardless of debt you must develop the habit of paying your wealth first and giving to charity.

It is worth repeating that there is an often heard fallacy that by investing in this way you are just waiting until you are too old to enjoy your money. Another way of looking at this is that the **slow growth** of wealth gives you immediate joy, let's you sleep better at night and leads to inspired decision making. People who create poor money habits and consistently squander whatever money they come in contact with also are prone to making bad decisions in other areas of their life. It has been proven again and again that to enjoy your life, you must live with **discipline**. Making short term sacrifices for long term gains gives you immediate feedback. You do not have to wait until you are too old to enjoy the pursuit of financial independence.

It is the habits we establish with our money that make all the difference. Do you remember the quote from the beginning of this book? It had to do with breaking bad habits but it is just as true for the habits that serve us:

> **"Chains of habit are too weak to be felt until they are too heavy to be broken."**
>
> **—Samuel Johnson**

It is common to wonder "How could I possibly live on 70% of my income, I can barely live on 110% of it now?" The next wealth ritual will answer that question...

Wealth Ritual Two: Be Frugal

The second ritual of wealth is to be frugal.

On living on a budget:

"Why are you going over your monthly expenses?...No, let me shorten this process for you: You make dog sh*t, so don't spend any money."

—Justin Halpern (Sh*t my dad says)

Spending less than you earn is a simple, fundamental key to financial independence. It is simple math: x dollars comes in and y dollars goes out. If you just make sure y is less than x and you're off to a good start. If you don't want to read on just understand, fully and completely, **most millionaires in this country are <u>very</u> frugal. Most of the people who drive expensive imports, wear expensive suits and live in expensive neighborhoods are not wealthy.**

Time is more valuable than money

It is worth noting that frugality is not the same as being cheap. Being frugal is deliberately and conscientiously getting the most value for every dollar spent. The most value, measured in the return on your investment in **time, energy and money**, might be the most expensive option in terms of money spent. When you approach life with a philosophy of frugality you are able to see things that others don't see. Sometimes pre-tested (used) items are really the best option.

"Time is more valuable than money. You can get more money, but you cannot get more time."

—Jim Rohn

Living Well Below Your Means

Think of the major categories you spend money on each month. Things like housing, food, entertainment, transportation and education instantly come to mind. Take food for instance. You can reduce your grocery bill by buying cheaper foods or you can reduce you overall food expense by adopting frugal habits. Habits like limiting the number of times you eat out and bringing lunch to work each day can drastically reduce your food expenditure while also improving the quality of food you eat. Buying fresh, locally grown produce in season can be an excellent frugal choice when compared to food bought from a restaurant.

Trying to lower your food bill or curb your energy consumption before you really evaluate what you are actually spending the most money on could be a mistake. Finding the biggest hole in the boat is critical, especially if you are sinking. Take a look at your monthly expenses and figure out which 2 or 3 have the most impact. You might be surprised.

Go Big or Go Home

For most Americans, the two biggest obstacles preventing financial independence is what they spend on **housing** and what they spend on **transportation**. If you can make huge progress in these two areas, everything else will fall neatly into place. On the flip side, you could watch every penny on every other expense besides these two and still fall way behind.

Housing

> **"A house is just a place to keep your stuff while you go out and get more stuff."**
>
> **—George Carlin**

There is some debate recently in the financial community as to whether owning a home is still a good investment. When so many families are underwater (mortgages exceeding home values) it is easy to argue that owning a home is a bad financial decision. I think right now is perhaps the best time to buy a home in a long, long time provided we are cognizant of value and do not allow our emotions to take control of our decisions. It is critical, though, to buy the right home for **you**. Your goal should be to find a decent home in a nice neighborhood, not your dream home in a posh neighborhood. There are many reasons for this.

Stop Acting Rich is the excellent follow-up to Thomas Stanley's bestselling book ***The Millionaire Next Door***. In it, Stanley further proves that there is a huge difference between *acting rich* and *being rich*. The **aspirationals**, as he calls them, do most of the luxury buying in this country but accumulate little wealth. Millionaires *really are* frugal.

> **"I believe the greatest detriment to building wealth is our home / neighborhood environment. If you live in a pricey home and neighborhood, you will act and buy like your neighbors."**
>
> **—Thomas J. Stanley (from *Stop Acting Rich*)**

When you live in an upscale neighborhood you need to accumulate the symbols of wealth, right? You certainly can't drive a Toyota or a Ford and you can't wear a Timex or a suit from J.C. Penney. Stanley proves through his research that millionaires indeed **do** wear Timex timepieces, drive Toyotas and buy modestly priced suits. Real millionaires are not concerned whatsoever with the Kardashians. What is striking from his study is that millionaires, by and large, are frugal.

Frugality Starts at Home

A significant component of the American Dream is home ownership. This has not changed. Many tax laws benefit homeowners and there are still several programs and incentives to help you purchase a home. Your home is at once a shelter from the rain and a shelter from high taxes. Many millionaires attribute a smart home purchase to their ability to accumulate wealth.

Any tax incentive needs to be carefully investigated. The biggest one, the **mortgage interest deduction**, seems like a good reason to buy a home but it is actually much smaller than you think. The only value of the mortgage interest deduction is the difference between **it** and the **standard deduction**. The decision to purchase a home should come from factors outside of financial perks or the promise of future gold.

There are a few simple guidelines to follow to make your dwelling arrangements a part of your financial growth. A happy home is one that is affordable through thick and thin. An extra bathroom or 1,000 more square feet is unimportant to a child who just wants a safe, warm place to spend time with mom and dad. You must be able to weather financial ups and downs. Becoming overextended with too much house during a financial crisis can be terrifying. Our economy is cyclical, there are boom times and bust times. We can weather the inevitable storms much better when we are in an appropriately priced home.

Millions of Americans, especially in recent years, have made the mistake of relying too heavily on things outside of their control in regards to their home purchase. They bought huge, expensive homes with the promise that the value would always go up and the payment would always be low. Homes don't always rise in value and interest rates can swing wildly making payments unpredictable and selling virtually impossible.

Return of the Starter Home

It once was that young families would work hard to save their money and put a down payment on a small, inexpensive property. This one act would allow them to more quickly pay off their mortgage and offered a whole bunch of additional benefits. Two major benefits of starter homes are that they cost you less and aid your frugality. Here is some more detail on these benefits:

Starter Homes Cost Less

1. **Lower purchase price:** A decent small house in a nice neighborhood costs less to buy and you'll pay much less in interest over the life of the loan.

2. **Lower taxes & Insurance**: These are based primarily on property value; lower value = lower taxes & insurance.

3. **Maintenance joy**: Less paint, fewer shingles and less time doing both activities makes home maintenance an enjoyable activity.

4. **Green Machine**: A small home is cheaper to initially insulate and a well-insulated small house continues to be cheaper to heat and cool.

Starter Homes Aid Stylish Frugality

1. **Smart decisions**: Less storage space actually forces good decisions about what is important. A big home is notorious for its ability to hide things from its owners. A small home pushes you to make

smarter decisions about what to keep and what to donate.

2. **Nice Furniture & Amenities**: Small space living encourages you to buy less frequently and with greater consideration of high-quality and long-lasting items. Beautiful wood flooring & granite countertops can be had for a fraction of the cost when you have fewer rooms and less square footage to cover.

Starter homes enhance the quality of life

All of these little things add up to a huge boost in the one thing that is thought to improve overall quality of life in recent years. *Time*. When you trade down to wealth in regards to choosing to live in a slightly smaller, more affordable home you reap all kinds of *time-related benefits*. You spend less time cleaning the house, less time working to pay the mortgage, utilities and taxes and less time and money on maintenance. Having more time freed up to pursue education, run a small side business and play with your kids cannot be underestimated.

One important note about buying a home: *Get a 30 year fixed rate mortgage, **Period***. Balloon, Adjustable Rate and Reverse mortgages are simply ways many people end up buying homes that are too expensive for them. These creative loans have a tendency to eat up your future equity and make your monthly payment unpredictable. You can sometimes get a lower interest rate by going with a 15 year term. It might make more sense to go with the 30 year and strive to pay it off in 15. Having a lower monthly mortgage *obligation* will come in handy if you fall on difficult times.

Buying a decent small house in a nice neighborhood will accelerate your ability to save and invest. A good decision here could be the best one you'll ever make.

When <u>Not</u> To Be a Homeowner

Even with the many advantages, home ownership is not for everyone. There are still a few good reasons to rent. The most compelling is the idea of mobility and career flexibility; does your career require frequent moves or travel? Perhaps having the flexibility that renting provides will be more beneficial.

You can still achieve financial independence without owning a home but you will need to remain steadfast in your investments. A 30 year fixed mortgage payment will be the same year after year; rents have a tendency to rise over time.

Whether to own a home or to rent depends on a variety of factors. Rents rise but so do the costs associated with home ownership. Do the math for your situation but keep in mind that the vast majority (98%) of millionaires, according Stanley's research, own their homes. (Stanley, Stop Acting Rich, 2009)

Vroom

What Americans spend on transportation is second only to housing. If you can drastically cut this expense you will be way ahead of the game. We love to drive and we love our cars. This fact is even more of a reason to be completely aware of this expense. Our choice of vehicle is a social marker. What we drive tells the world who we are and what we value. The American car embodies 100 years of status. Our entire society is built with the automobile as a prominent actor both socially and financially. There would be no **suburbs** if not for the rise of the great American car.

Especially early on, if you can forego the need to drive an expensive car you will free up tons of resources for real wealth building. Think of the people *you* like and admire. Does the hunk of metal and plastic in their driveway factor in **at all** in your estimation of them? What really is the difference between a Toyota and a Lexus, a Chevy and a Cadillac? Surprisingly little! Luxury car makers use the same engines and transmissions in their high end brands as their low cost cousins.

I hate to pick on a single car manufacturer but I think this is especially eye opening. Mercedes has been for a long time the epitome of luxury. They have more recently become an example of **not** getting what you pay for. Mercedes cars have shown a steady decline in reliability ratings (according to Consumer Reports) for several years. Combined with the **Millionaire Next Door** data, it looks as if Mercedes knows its target audience, **aspirationals** who want to *look* rich rather than *be* rich. They have succeeded in selling a nameplate on an unreliable car at a premium price. This is sad. Quality is secondary to the illusion of opulence for the **aspirationals**.

Reliability Costs Less

In the automobile arena, quality really does cost less. Total cost of ownership of a vehicle has many factors. The top 3 are exactly what you would expect: Initial cost, fuel economy and reliability. I would like to stress that one of these is far more important, **Reliability**. The cost of an undependable car is far more than just the price of the repairs. Time is more valuable than money, as we have said, and dealing with a broken down car is a time consuming, frustrating experience. Choose a reliable, inexpensive car that will get you where you need to go and you will sidestep one of the most prolific drains on wealth ever created.

Rent your fun

Many times what we think will be a fun, lifelong endeavor turns out to be a passing fancy. Variety is the spice of life, it is said, and too often we buy a current variety only to find that the spice wears out over time.

What then? We have to store, maintain, repair and pay taxes on the thing that was supposed to be a fun experiment. Let's take a look at two examples.

Vacation Home

The mythology of the vacation home is an enduring fantasy. A cabin in the woods or a bungalow on the beach is a romantic ideal. The truth of the matter is somewhat disappointing. You end up paying for something all year that you rarely use and when you do get a chance to escape you have all sorts of maintenance, paperwork and stresses to deal with, **on vacation**. When you are off vacation you might be reminded of the additional overhead that a vacation home represents. *Did you remember to pay the HOA dues? Did you turn off the water; the pipes will freeze if you forgot.* Instead of buying a vacation home try to save for a great vacation in an exotic location. You'll find in most cases that it will be cheaper to rent your fun.

Whatever Floats Your Boat

In Andrew Tobias's book, **The Only Investment Guide You'll Ever Need**, he advises on what to do if you inherit a fortune. He makes it a point to say "**do not buy a boat**". This is great advice and I wish I had taken it sooner. In my defense, I inherited a small sailboat and it then proceeded to inherit my vast fortune (which, at the time, was luckily miniscule). In boats as it is in vacation properties, it makes financial sense to rent your fun.

Every major body of water has a boat rental. Every major city in the world has a place where you can rent a convertible for the weekend or a motorcycle or Jet-Ski for the day. If you really want to experience the thrill of speed or watersports you can do so for very little money. You can even learn to fly a fighter jet for less than you would spend in two months on a luxury car. **It is the experiences in life that we remember and cherish, not the ownership.**

Frugality is a philosophy of value

Thinking frugally allows us to look at what something costs us over a period of years, not just **per month** or **right now**. Thinking of the total cost of everything you buy will help you make much better decisions with your money. The long term Total Cost of Ownership (TCO) has many factors. There are costs associated to storing and maintaining. There are costs associated to repairing and replacing. Sometimes paying more for a product that is of superior quality and reliability is the best choice. Quality usually costs less when evaluated in terms of TCO.

The philosophy of value has another component as well. Value is personal. It does not matter if the product is the most valuable product in its class if it is not **valuable to you**. Trying to impress our peers is possibly the biggest drain on wealth there is.

Thrift, frugality and spending less than you earn are sometimes ridiculed as being cheap. *Spendy* family or friends might call you a tightwad or a cheapskate. Welcome comments like that as evidence of your success. It is important to remember that millionaires consistently rank among the most frugal and thrifty persons in our society. It is easy to mistake the accoutrements of wealth for actual wealth and many often do. The statistics are overwhelming. Wealthy persons rarely own new luxury cars and they tend to seek out good deals on everything they buy.

Nothing about our financial life is rational. Our decisions are emotional. Our values, beliefs and our sense of purpose determine our decisions. Can we have good values and make bad decisions? ***Of course***! Even the smallest transaction is a complex sequence of events and we may overlook an important detail. We must do our research, take action and learn from our successes as well as our mistakes.

Summary

If we can tackle to two biggest drains on our wealth accumulation, *transportation* and *housing,* we are off to a great start. These big choices will trickle down and affect many areas of our lives. A smaller, more manageable home is less costly to heat, cool, repair and insure. A low cost reliable car has similar cost saving benefits.

Approaching our lives with a philosophy of value is knowing that being frugal is not about sacrifice but rather is a rewarding and enjoyable way of life. Being frugal frees up more money where it makes the most impact, our financial independence.

Wealth Ritual Three: Be Your Own Boss

> **"Entrepreneurs and their small enterprises are responsible for almost all the economic growth in the United States."**
>
> **—Ronald Reagan**

To be your own boss means to take full ownership of your destiny. The great promise of America does not, as we have seen recently, mean owning a McMansion, two luxury cars and a Jet Ski but rather the opportunity to pursue your dreams. **Dreams matter**. They always have and they always will. Forging into solid existence an idea is the path of the entrepreneur.

The lifelong career of the American worker is long gone. No longer can anyone rely on a corporation or government to take their hand at graduation and lead them to retirement. Most people will have 7-10 jobs throughout their working life. These jobs could span several different careers. It is evident that being a lifelong learner is essential to stay employed and relevant within a rapidly changing global marketplace.

One way to become and to stay valuable, even if you plan on working in a field that requires employment in a large organization, is to learn to think like an entrepreneur.

The Adventure of the Entrepreneur

We have all heard that small business is the backbone of our economy. Did you know that small business accounts for over half of the private sector jobs and over half of nonfarm GDP (gross domestic product) in America? The American dream is predicated on opportunity and nothing embodies that spirit more than the adventure of the entrepreneur.

Some enterprises seem to be buoyed entirely by a good idea, despite the owner's mismanagement. Others are long shots that prevail only through the tenacity and bullheadedness of the person in charge. One thing is almost always certain; it is the marketplace that decides the fate of the enterprise.

Starting and running your own business can be risky. The odds are stacked against you and the hard truth is that most businesses fail. Even good, well-crafted and well run businesses fail. This risk threshold prevents many from ever trying. What is not immediately evident in the failure statistics is what becomes of the entrepreneur whose business did not succeed. The skills you acquire in starting and running your own enterprise do not disappear with a business closure.

When an enterprise is created based on passion, talent and skill, the odds of success increase tremendously. Everyone needs to consider starting and running their own business.

What is the best way to start and run a home based business?

Do what you are.

Do you like to fix things or solve problems? Do you want greatly to heal people or animals? Do you like to create original works of art? Do like to perform or create music? Do you like to clean things, break things or repair things? Do you enjoy writing or speaking to groups? Do you like to create computer programs that bring people together? Successful businesses have been built on these and many other areas. Remember, it is not the business but rather the consistent habits and rituals of the business owner that predict success or failure of an enterprise.

By choosing a business that is aligned with your calling, your vocation becomes much more rewarding. You are your business; your purpose and passion become the basis for your success.

Your business

Your business must be aligned with your purpose and values. One of the often overlooked reasons a business may fail is that the business owner was not even interested in the product or service he was selling. Seldom will a business succeed if it is begun for love of money. In fact, when you make your passion into a business, the activities you engage in to grow your enterprise are many times rewarding in and of themselves. Being engaged in the activities of serving others with your unique talents and gifts makes good business sense. What makes owning and running a small business so appealing?

1. You have the ability to do what you are passionate about. Your business can be based on your passion. Becoming an expert in something you love is much easier than trying to force someone else's idea of a money-making idea.

2. You have unlimited financial opportunity. Your income is only limited by your ability to adapt to the demands of your customers.

3. You are the decision maker. This is the freedom part. You are the decider, the commander in chief. There is great pressure to make the right choice but there is awesome freedom in being in the position to make this decision. Choice is better than no choice. Strive to be a decision maker.

4. You are involved in every part of the business. You can focus on what ties into your strengths and offload (delegate) those things that don't. If this all seems daunting remember that you can learn all of these skills from your SCORE mentor, SBA Smart Start and from the books I recommend.

5. **You can take advantage of enormous tax benefits**. As we will see, there are two tax systems at work in America, one for employees and one for business owners. One is better (by a long shot). Guess which one it is.

> *"You can only become truly accomplished at something you love. Don't make money your goal. Instead, pursue the things you love doing, and then do them so well that people can't take their eyes off you."*
>
> —*Maya Angelou*

The two tax systems

Despite what you may have been lured to believe in the recent political debates, taxes are good. Taxes are simply the dues we pay to enjoy the great boons that government provides for our society. We should enjoy paying taxes and take pride in what our ability to pay gives to us. Taxes provide for the national defense and they provide a safety net to catch the unfortunate souls who, for reasons that could affect any of us, free-fall into helplessness. We are owners of our society; free people in a free society. It is our duty both civic and moral, to provide for the common good.

> *"All I'm saying is that when everything has been computed, all legitimate deductions have been taken, and you reach that last line on your income tax form, whatever the amount, pay it. And pay with happiness, knowing that you're feeding the goose that lays the golden eggs-the golden eggs of freedom, safety, justice, and free*

enterprise. Some goose! Some eggs!

– Jim Rohn

We could complain about paying taxes and grumble about how unfair it is or we could adopt Jim Rohn's philosophy and become a "**Happy Taxpayer**" (Rohn, 1999). I suggest that if you paid taxes last year you should be thankful. Millions of people around the world could not pay taxes to their government, state or their municipality. They in turn could not visit a library, could not drive on a paved road, could not drink clean water, nor could they call a paramedic or a firefighter. We must never let those who serve us get carried away with their power and we need to hold all elected officials accountable but we also must understand that taxes are a financial vessel that propels our society forward.

While it is important to become willing participants in the good of our society, it is equally important that we *pay no more than our duty requires*. It is our civic duty to remain a viable contributor to society and not to **overpay** our taxes.

There are two distinct tax systems in America, a system for employees and a system for business. If you are an employee you pay taxes on your wages or salary. There are advantages to being an employee and most people, even business owners, are employees at times throughout their work life. In the employee tax system you earn a salary or a wage and then these are taxed. You can reduce the amount you are taxed slightly by donating to charity, paying mortgage interest and a few other things.

Employee Tax

(Gross income – Taxes) = Net income

Employees are taxed on their earnings

The second and preferable tax system is that of business. Business is taxed on **profits**, not income. Business tax kicks in after you have subtracted all of the expenses of your business.

Business Tax

(Gross income — Expenses) = Net income

Business is taxed on net income

Commonly deducted business expenses:

Computer equipment
Legal services
Accounting services
Business related meals
Vehicle use or depreciation
Home office use
Books
Education
Business related travel

Small business is the economic engine of our country. Tax laws are favorable to small business in many ways and that is as it should be. It is the thousands of small businesses across our country that provides opportunity and growth for so many.

Small business owners are the captains of their destinies. They enjoy tax benefits employees could only dream of. Former IRS attorney Sandy Botkin says in his book, **Lower Your Taxes - Big Time!**, that "*you would be brain dead not to start a home-based business.*" (In fact that is the title of the first chapter). Things such as membership dues, entertaining clients and business related travel are all deductible. If your business is built on your passion then you are able to **do what you are**, **serve others** with your talents and **enjoy the tax benefits that accompany it**.

It is critical that you run your business **as a business** (and not a hobby). It is the top weapon of the IRS to treat a small business as a hobby and to disallow deductions. Forming an LLC and keeping excellent records (as outlined in **Lower Your Taxes – Big Time!**) will ensure that your business is not seen by the IRS as a hobby.

Rocket Fuel for your Venture

> **"The business schools reward difficult complex behavior more than simple behavior, but simple behavior is more effective."**
>
> **—Warren Buffet**

It does not take an enormous amount of formal education to be successful at business. Pursuing higher education and advanced degrees are important for many fields and are becoming more important in the job market but you just don't need an MBA to run a profitable business.

There are excellent resources out there that you can take advantage of to learn how to run a successful enterprise.

The Small Business Administration (SBA) can propel you off to a successful start. They offer training, financial assistance and even assistance selling your product or service to the federal government. You can learn about how to set up your business, business accounting and marketing for instance all at your local Small Business Development Center (SBDC).

As we discussed in the section on mentoring, it is worth repeating that you should take a look at SCORE. In partnership with the SBA, SCORE provides free mentoring services to entrepreneurs. **SCORE, the Counselors to America's Small Business** is comprised of over 100,000 volunteers from every industry. It is an amazing resource for anyone thinking of starting a business and even for seasoned veterans who find themselves stuck in some way.

Am I the entrepreneur type?

Let's be clear. It is not necessary to own and run your own business to become financially independent. You can develop and utilize the habits of wealth either with a job or as an entrepreneur (or both). **Thinking like an entrepreneur** is the key. There are no hard rules on what it takes to be a successful business owner but there are two important distinctions:

1. Employees care about **execution**, entrepreneurs care about **results**.
2. Employees focus on **salary**, entrepreneurs on **profit**.

Thinking like an entrepreneur has the added benefit of making you a more appreciated employee. Focusing on profit and results rather than execution and salary shows your employer that you are interested in the success of the enterprise, not just the task at hand.

Let's think about what type of business would potentially be the right one for us.

Exercises

Within your vocation and passion are the seeds to a successful business.

1. How can I help others by doing what I am?

2. What product or service can I provide that is in alignment with my talents, interests, desires and skills?
3. What am I really good at that I can share with others?
4. What business skills do I currently have?
5. What business skills am I committed to learn over the next 12 months?

We have learned so far to pay our wealth first, to be frugal and to embrace entrepreneurship. This is primarily playing offense. The next wealth ritual is concerned more with defense...

Wealth Ritual Four: Cover Your Assets

Bad things happen to good people. Bad people prey on good people. You need to be prepared for both. Having the right kind of Insurance and the appropriate business structure are needed to protect yourself and your family from unnecessary risk.

Umbrella Insurance

Lawsuits are everywhere. Judges are awarding larger amounts of money than ever before. Most homeowner policies have a limit on how much is covered. If an unfortunate accident should happen that is determined to be your fault, a judge could find you negligent and award the victims an **ungodly** amount of money. As your financial assets grow, you need to make sure you are adequately protected. Umbrella insurance used to be a tool for the wealthy; it is now a needed protection for every policyholder. The good news is that an umbrella policy is cheap; you can get a $1 million policy for $250-$500 a year through the same company that offers you homeowners insurance. It is well worth it!

Business structure

Many new home-based businesses can and should be set up as a sole proprietorship. As your business grows and you take on more responsibility and risk, shifting to a Limited Liability Company might be appropriate. We'll briefly cover both and offer a few steps to get your business started.

Sole Proprietorship

Most home based businesses can be formed as a Sole Proprietorship with relatively little risk. There are some great advantages to this form of business. Possible exceptions are if you are starting a business that exposes you to high liability or debt because in a Sole Proprietorship, *you are one in the same with the business* and assume complete responsibility for liabilities and debts.

The three biggest advantages to this type of business structure are the low barriers to entry (and exit). A sole proprietorship is easy to start, easy to run and easy to upgrade to an LLC when the time is right.

Easy to Start

Decide on a name and obtain the necessary business licenses and permits for your business. The Small Business Administration has excellent, free online courses in this area. They also have courses on preparing a business plan, business accounting, marketing and other key startup concerns. Don't underestimate the usefulness of these excellent resources.

Easy to Run

Sole proprietors are in complete control and can make decisions as they see fit. Profits from the business flow directly to the owner's personal tax return. Bookkeeping is straightforward and there are some excellent tools on the market to assist the Sole Proprietor run a lean and successful enterprise.

Easy to Upgrade

The business is easy to dissolve and somewhat easy to upgrade to an LLC when it becomes necessary.

Limited Liability Company

If the business you engage in has a higher exposure to risk, it might be a good idea to form an LLC. Limited liability companies make the business entity liable for claims and damages, not necessarily the business owner. One of the major reasons LLCs are formed in Nevada is not the tax savings but rather the extra liability shield that state provides. (Botkin, 2011) In some cases, taxes can be higher but for businesses that need extra protection; it can be well worth it. In any event, proper insurance and ethical business practices are your best defense.

Important reasons you may want to form an LLC:

1. LLC owners have limited liability for business debts and obligations.
2. LLCs can have multiple owners and may issue shares of stock to attract outside investors.
3. LLC owners can report the profits and losses of their business on their personal tax returns.

Ask your mentor

The mentor you choose in your area of expertise can be extremely helpful in this regard. Many of them have run successful businesses and understand the opportunities and pitfalls you are likely to encounter. If you are interested in forming an LLC I highly recommend picking up a copy of Jennifer Reuting's book, **Limited Liabilities for Dummies,** or just going to her site, MyLLC.com and set one up.

Even if you decide not to go into business or form an LLC, it is still a great idea to get the extra coverage that umbrella insurance provides. Above all, if you are not certain that what you are doing is both legal and ethical, don't do it!

Here are a few actions to take to begin to **cover your assets**:

1. **If your employer offers it, spring for the additional long-term disability insurance.** Usually just a few dollars a paycheck and will come in handy if you become disabled and cannot work for a long period of time.

2. **Make sure you have the right amount of homeowners insurance.** You need to make sure the benefit will be enough to replace your home at current costs for materials and labor.

3. **Make sure your contingency fund is in an FDIC (Federal Deposit Insurance Corporation) insured account.** Getting a few extra percentage points from a shaky non-bank is not worth the risk.

4. **Buy Term Life insurance and invest the difference.** This old adage is as true today as it was many years ago. Whole or Universal life insurance does not match term life **plus** smart index fund investments.

Wealth Ritual Five: Live with an Attitude of Gratitude

Thanks!

Gratitude is one of the most important aspects of a healthy life. Being grateful is an acknowledgement that you have received a gift and that you appreciate the intentions of the gift-giver. In his book *Thanks!*, Dr. Robert Emmons, Professor of Psychology at UC Davis, explains why it is so good to be grateful. **"When people regularly engage in the systematic cultivation of gratitude, they experience a variety of measurable benefits...people who practice gratitude are measurably happier and are more pleasant to be around."** (Emmons PH.D, 2008)

> *"The mental attitude of gratitude draws the mind into closer touch with the source from which the blessings come."*
>
> **—Wallace Wattles**

Being grateful for what you have is a necessary habit to develop. Engaging in charity is one of the best ways to express gratitude. We have already decided that the 3rd dime from every dollar will go to charity.

Charity

Charity is giving help to people who are not related to you. Charitable giving can be money, goods or personal time and effort. It can be directly to the needy or to an organization that helps them. It can be to a church that helps the poor in a community or to a science lab that is attempting to find a cure for a disease. Visiting the elderly or helping build a home for a poor family are acts of charity.

Remember to start where you are and give what you can. Give your time, effort and energy if you have little money. Identify people in your community who are at risk and help them.

Ask yourself the following questions:

1. What am I grateful for in my life?
2. When can I give thanks to my creator every day? In the shower? On a jog or a walk?
3. What is a *cause* that I feel strongly about?
4. Who in my community could use some help? How can I help them?
5. What can I do to help others who are suffering or struggling?

An often ignored cure for moderate to mild depression is to simply stop focusing on ourselves and instead to focus on how we can help others. Depression, inevitably, cannot survive when we focus on the happiness, welfare and general care of others. We need to get outside of ourselves to truly appreciate the joy of contribution.

When we live with gratitude it also creates an attractive force in our life. This is not anything mystical or weird (as some people would have you believe). Living with gratefulness forces our focus outside ourselves and allows us to appreciate things we would not normally see. People are naturally attracted to grateful people. There is presupposed joy and confidence in a person who expresses gratitude and that is easy to detect.

The Road of Trials

"Once having traversed the threshold, the hero moves in a dream landscape of curiously fluid, ambiguous forms, where he must survive a succession of trials." (Campbell, The Hero With a Thousand Faces, 1949)

Once firmly on the road to wealth and fulfillment, obstacles seem to appear from almost everywhere. In our own lives, it may seem that things are thrown at us in ways that we cannot handle. We **can** handle them. It is our response to the challenges of life that define who we are and what we are truly capable of. Some people will let you down. Some small-minded people will try to hurt you, trick you and take things from you. It is the frame you place around these events in your life that give them meaning, that give them power. You give these events the power to destroy you or the power to give your life more meaning.

It is not what happens to us that matters, it is how we assign meaning to what happens to us that matters. We are all here for a reason; we have a life to live and a purpose to fulfill.

Our shield from the trials of life is our character and our sword to defeat any enemy is our perseverance.

The Six Pillars of Character

In the book **Making Ethical Decisions**, former law professor Michael Josephson describes the six pillars of character. His organization, Character Counts, teaches these 6 ethical values to youth groups and businesses. The six pillars of a person's character are **trustworthiness, respect, responsibility, fairness, caring and**

citizenship. (Josephson, 2002)Striving to live with each of these values is the best way to build a strong character.

The word **character** in its original Greek meant the mark impressed upon a coin. Our character is made up of the markings that have been etched upon us throughout our lives. Character has little to do with intelligence or education. We all have heard of highly educated criminals and intellectually gifted crooks. Character is made up of the small decisions we make every day that allow us to live up to our values. Our character is diminished when we choose to do things that violate our values and is strengthened when we strive to live up to our highest ideals.

"We must remember that intelligence is not enough. Intelligence plus character - that is the goal of true education."

–Martin Luther King Jr.

A simple way to look at character is to ponder this question: **What would I be willing to do to help others even if I knew no one else would ever know about it?** Sometimes what smells like character is really pride, avarice or greed. An example related to charity highlights this. Giving to obtain a tax benefit or free publicity does indeed still help the recipients but it does not add much to your character. Character is the quiet confidence of a job well done.

Fix your regrets

Nobody's perfect. There are probably more than a few things we have done in our life that have taken away from our character. We do things we are not proud of, sometimes more often than we would like to admit. We may have done things that hurt another person. Sometimes we hurt others by mistake, other times we hurt others out of anger or fear. We may even feel justified in the actions we took.

> **"We crucify ourselves between two thieves: regret for yesterday and fear of tomorrow."**
>
> **—Fulton Oursler**

Fixing your regrets is about going back in time, identifying the people we may have hurt in some way and apologizing to them.

I'm Sorry

Acknowledging that you have hurt another person and taking responsibility for your actions is one true test of a hero. This will not erase the event and may not heal the pain that they suffered but it is important for you to build your character. Expressing remorse to others for your actions affirms your strength and restores your dignity. It is a single act that works within the realm of all six pillars of your character.

In mythology, the Hero's word was sufficient for all agreements. Your word must be as valuable. Your word should be your bond.

> **"Happiness is when what you think, what you say, and what you do are in harmony."**
>
> **—Mohandas K. Gandhi**

Perseverance

The world is full of starters. Strong starters who get excited about an idea, motivated to act and who expend a ton of resources in the early stages. When any idea or project reaches a certain stage, there is resistance. This could be a newly found awareness that the project would be more difficult to complete than anticipated. It could be an external force providing a setback. There may need to be a special license or tool that was not identified and now needs to be obtained. In any endeavor, there is a balance between planning and acting. If the planning stage is taken to the extreme there can be **analysis paralysis**, a state of over planning that has a tendency to shut down motivation before you even begin. On the other hand, zero planning and research is also a recipe for disaster. So what is the right combination?

> *The great majority of men are*
> *bundles of beginnings.*
>
> *–Ralph Waldo Emerson*

We learned earlier that there is no failure, only learning. Failure itself is simply how we learn to do things. Sometimes we assign a value to the end state of a task and not to the task itself, that is, we want the results without the effort. We want the rewards but not the problems. While we are learning to do what we are we will invariably make mistakes, sometimes costly ones. We must accept these as learning experiences and try again. There will be times when the going gets tough, problems seem insurmountable and we just want to quit. These are the times when we must persist. We must latch onto our worthy goal and continue.

The hero must see it through to the end. The road of trials is designed to test his resolve. Each enemy he faces along the way is another opportunity to learn, grow and become stronger. Within each failure and setback is a seed of opportunity. He must plan well and persevere until he finishes his noble task.

Defeat the Five Enemies of Wealth

Financial challenges are an inevitable part of growth. These challenges are made up of the poor habits that we engage in and enemies that want to take advantage of us.

A fool and his money are soon parted.

—Thomas Tusser

It is when we first start to engage in the pursuit of opportunity that we are the most vulnerable. We are vulnerable to our own fears, the whims of experts and to the call of easy money. It is when we start to make headway and succeed that we fall victim to ourselves. There are five enemies that it would be wise to confront before you begin your journey.

The Five Enemies of Wealth:

Enemy One: **The Fear of Risk**

Enemy Two: **The Dozers**

Enemy Three: **The Aspirationals**

Enemy Four: **The Sirens of Debt**

Enemy Five: **Beware the Guru**

Enemy One: The Fear of Risk

All life is risk. We have been at risk since the day we were born. The biggest risk most of us face, however, is living our life without taking any.

Some of us were born into hazardous environments while others are bounded by safety and security. Both environments have risk. There is risk in the things we choose to do. There is also a more severe risk of doing nothing. Some of us are forced to face risk at an early age; others are protected from risk well into adulthood.

It is important to note that high risk is not always synonymous with high reward. Gambling, for instance, is high risk with very little chance of reward. You will rarely see a casino owner at the gambling table. Lotteries, even state run lotteries are absurdly high risk with a miniscule chance of reward.

> *"Lottery: A tax on people who are bad at math."*
>
> *—Author Unknown*

Taking risks is not an inherent virtue. Risk taking alone can be devastating to oneself and one's family. Choosing the appropriate risks to take and going for the rewards they shield can produce life's biggest accomplishments. Risk should be considered in areas where you must stretch yourself to fulfill them. There will be times when you will need to put it on the line.

> *"Man cannot discover new oceans unless he has the courage to lose sight of the shore."*
>
> *—Andre Gide*

Unlimited Opportunity, Unlimited Risk

When you take the helm of your own ship and set sail, the entire ocean awaits. There are no boundaries, no limits. The only limits of your opportunity exist in your imagination. Risk lies on the other side of the coin of opportunity. They exist together always. We must do our research, explore the upside and the downside and then be willing to act. Nothing happens unless we act. Walls cannot fall until we first swing the hammer. There is a time in the journey of the hero when the entire adventure hinges on a single decision. It is in these moments that the hero must be bold in order to be triumphant.

> **"One cannot leap a twenty foot chasm in two ten foot jumps."**
>
> **—American proverb**

How to Defeat the Fear of Risk

The key to beating the fear of risk is not to take them blindly. The primary way to mitigate risk in business, investing and in life is through education. Become immersed in the subject at hand. Learn everything you can about your business or subject. The more you know about the endeavor, the less real risk there is. With education, the reward stays the same while the level of risk drops. Warren Buffet does not risk his money in the stock market; he invests in companies that he has thoroughly studied. He reads everything he can (especially the intensely boring annual reports) looking for signs of a bargain. By the time he pulls the trigger, there is very little risk left in the equation.

> **"Risk comes from not knowing what you're doing."**
>
> **—Warren Buffet**

Beta

"Beta", in Wall Street speak, is the measure of volatility compared to the overall market. A high beta accelerates earnings when an investment is doing well and accelerates losses when the investment tanks. I like to think of beta as **magnitude**. When you put your money, time or energy in something it tends to magnify the results, positive or negative. If that something happens to be an investment, business opportunity or purchase that you have **thoroughly researched** then your actual risk goes down. People who put all of their investment eggs into a single basket can see incredible gains. They can also see incredible losses. Education and research changes this equation in your favor.

Immigrant Song

Why is it that a person, in the most desperate situation, can come to America and thrive when another person receiving a stipend, every conceivable advantage and first-hand knowledge of the native language and culture can fail miserably? What is the difference? Knowing that someone will be there with a net and a bag of money if you fail can feel great to one and be disheartening to another. People need to have a consequence for inaction and mistakes. Without the risk of failure or pain, success is stripped of its nectar. The dry-cleaner succeeds because there is no other option. Knowing there is *no return* can be the best motivation of all.

The Greatest Risk

It is easy to forget in our lives that we are here for a very short time. When we are young the days seem to last forever. As adults we sometimes see our days as obstacles to our weekends and we watch our kids grow up too fast. Days, weeks and months streak by at an accelerating rate. When we summon the courage to disengage from the current that propels us, we can choose the opportunities that are right for us.

"If you don't risk anything, you risk even more."

—Erica Jong

Many of the things that make life worthwhile are the challenges we face. A life of ease, while at the top of the list for many people, never made anyone happy. Happiness comes from confronting challenge, overcoming obstacles, growing, learning and becoming more than we are.

"To win without risk is to triumph without glory."

—Pierre Corneille 1636

Enemy Two: The Dozers

In the late 1800s the term "bull-dose" meant enough medicine to knock out a bull. It was later adapted to heavy, tank-like machinery that could plow through just about any obstacle. A bulldozer could plow through anything. For our purposes, the various dozers we discuss are chiefly concerned with plowing through your money. Once set off, a bulldozer goes and goes until there is nothing left in its path. If your house or car happens to be in the way then it was *game over*.

Meet the Dozers

There are three major dozers that present a hazard to your financial life and just like a bulldozer they can do significant damage. The dozers that present the most threat to your financial well-being are:

The HouseDozer
The StockDozer
The DollarDozer

The HouseDozer

There was a time when real estate was considered the best investment in the world. Home prices were rising, there were tax breaks to be had and if it came time to sell, you could make a tidy profit on your investment in a matter of weeks. In certain areas there were bidding wars that further drove up your profit. Buying a house, no matter what the cost, was a no-brainer. Real estate was a sure thing, until *it wasn't*.

All of the sudden it came to an end. People were losing their jobs. Homes, the sure thing of the economy, were getting foreclosed on. Home values plummeted and the housing boom was over.

We know now that loose regulation allowed banks to profit even if the homeowner could not repay the loan. The banks would make a subprime loan out the front door and sell a security (blessed by the ratings agencies as 'safe') out the back door. People were increasingly jumping on board and buying homes that they could never afford.

If all your money was in the real estate chair when the music stopped, the **HouseDozer** wiped you out.

The StockDozer

Stock crashes have been observed all the way back to 1720 when the Mississippi Company failed and Banque Royale stopped payment causing economic collapse in France.

The most notable stock decline was the stock panic of 1929 which led to the Great Depression.

The recent economic collapse, just like in 1929, was almost impossible to predict. It hit hard and fast and wiped out huge amounts of accumulated wealth. Even in a strong overall economy individual companies can fail rendering their stock worthless.

If you work for a company and own its stock your risk is even higher. Invest in **Stock Index Funds** and **Bond Index Funds**. If something unexpected happens to the company you work for, you have not only lost your job but also your wealth. Diversify!

The DollarDozer

If the StockDozer is enough to keep you from investing in the market, consider the alternative, **The Dollar Dozer**, or as it is commonly called **inflation**. Inflation means that tomorrow's dollar buys less stuff than today's dollar can. Having a million dollars when you retire sounds great to anyone unless you realize that a Chevy in 2050

(40 years from now) could cost you a significant chunk of that million.

In 1970 a Chevy pickup was about $2500 and a gallon of gas was 36 cents. A new house would cost you about $25,000. An 8 track tape player for your car, the epitome of sound sophistication at the time, went for about 40 dollars. Before you hop into the Delorean and take a trip back remember that the average income was under $10,000 per year.

How Do I defeat The Dozers?

The sure way to defeat the dozers is to make sure that you are **diversified and invested in the Whole Market**. Diversification keeps you from losing everything if one stock or bond should fail and investing in the whole market means that your wealth will grow as the greater market grows.

Enemy Three: The Aspirationals

Conspicuous consumption is one of the most insidious destroyers of wealth most people face. The Aspirationals represent the cardinal opposite of the ritual of frugality but deserve special mention. Your spending habits are the outward manifestation of your values. In our effort to carve out an identity and fit into the world around us we develop rituals of spending that can be hazardous to our future.

Invidious

Invidious consumption is a form of consumption intended to make others envious. We all want nice things, to feel significant in some way. It is when our material desires outstrip our capability to furnish them that we get into severe trouble.

The Consumption Spiral

The accoutrements of wealth represent symbols of status without the underlying capital to support them. It is an outward cry to establish one's own significance. Once this habit is started it is difficult to break. Imported handbags, luxury cars and expensive wines beget other even more expensive items and habits. Luxury homes need to be furnished. Gadgets need to be the smallest and the fastest. When our identities are formed around the consumer goods we own, it becomes difficult to stay relevant to our peers without buying newer and better things.

Eliminate the illusion of wealth pressure from your peers.

Our friends, neighbors and family have an enormous impact on this. Sometimes just having an open and honest conversation with your good friends can be curative. Others are not so willing to comply. Once you make wealth a must it is much easier to stick with your plan. It might take a while for these people to be convinced of your sincerity, but you must persevere.

Don't be an early adopter

Newly released technology is usually obscenely overpriced. When a person buys the product in this stage they are paying early adopter tax. What's more, Technical products malfunction more often and tend to have more problems and less features in the early part of their lifecycle. It is not uncommon to see lines form down the street for the first crack at a new and exciting product.

In fashion, a trendsetter or lighthouse customer is the early adopter. Paying many times the price people pay just a few months later when the product is green lighted for production. With just a little ingenuity and patience you can be fashionable and trendy without destroying your wealth. Sometimes, our identity is so closely tied to the things we own that upon further inspection, we realize that these things actually own us. They have such an impressive hold over our identity that just the thoughts of going without them makes us feel uncomfortable. It is important to unwind the things we have from the person that we are.

Trade down to wealth

If you are a conspicuous consumer you probably winced at even the thought of this. You must consider the alternative. It is likely that you are financing an unsustainable lifestyle with after-tax dollars. Most luxury items are extremely poor investments. Realize that it is very possible to be stylishly frugal. Most people will not even notice.

1. What things to I have that really define me as a person? Who would I be if I did not have these things?

2. What can I stop spending money on that will minimally impact my lifestyle?
3. Who are my *"illusion of wealth"* friends?
4. In what major areas will I trade down to wealth?

Enemy Four: The Sirens of Debt

The beautiful sirens persuaded passing mariners to linger among the sharp rocks. The island where the sirens lived was littered with the bones of the dead.

Banks summon us with beautiful song. *Have whatever you want, right now.* Anything money can buy is within your grasp. Credit is necessary for a good life.

> **"We must steer clear of the Sirens, their enchanting song, their meadow starred with flowers."**
>
> **—Homer – (The Odyssey)**

Consumer debt is self-imposed slavery. It is the archenemy of wealth creation. By borrowing money to pay for consumer products you destroy your future earnings and kill off any hope of real wealth. Consumption before earning is a dangerous lie. It hurts you. Eliminating the debt you already have accumulated is one of the *rituals of wealth,* ensuring that you avoid racking up future debt is the key here.

Face the Music

One way to come to grips with how destructive the sirens can be is to go into the place where you keep the things you no longer use. For some it is the garage, others an attic or spare room. *How many of the things collecting dust and taking up space were necessities when you bought them with that credit card? What are they worth now?* If you are not using them then they are worth **less than zero to you**. Not only are you not getting any utility or use out of the item, you are still paying interest on the loan you used to buy it.

Go On a Saving Spree

As we learned earlier, willpower is a muscle. Start small and build up your power to *not spend*. Go to the mall and buy nothing. Empty your online shopping carts. Go to your favorite store and walk out without a bag or a box. Spend nothing. When you see something you want to buy and make a conscious decision not to buy it, your willpower gets a little bit stronger.

Transaction Abstraction

Buying stuff is made up of tons of brain activity. There are, however, a few areas of the brain that seem to battle over the decision to buy. The **nucleus accumbens** gets activated when we see something we like. When we see how much it costs our **insula** kicks in and our **mesial prefrontal cortex** (**MPFC**) shuts down. This battle of opposites happens whenever we make a decision to by something. (Knutsen, Rick, Wimmer, Drazen, & Loewenstein, 2007).

When you throw credit into the mix it knocks this decision-making system off balance. Paying with a credit card activates the **nucleus accumbens** while the **insula** and **MPFC** remains unmoved.

> **"The abstract nature of credit coupled with deferred payment may "anaesthetize" consumers against the pain of paying"** **(Prelec & loewenstein, 1998)**

Our brains just don't get credit cards. Cut them up or at the very least **don't bring them with you to the store. People make much better purchasing decisions with cash.**

Having credit available tends to make you forget the long term cost of using it and only focus on the short term pleasure of having something now. Credit availability distorts a person's ability to budget, get informed and make good buying decisions. Committing to only buy things with *money you have already earned* is a powerful habit. It keeps you aware of the real value of money.

How do you defeat the sirens of debt?

1. **Pay Cash:** When paying cash to buy something, people tend to make much better choices, do much more research and comparison shopping and most importantly are happier with the results both immediately and over time.

2. **Create a 2 week wait list:** Write the item, its price and todays date on a list and only buy the item after two weeks have passed. Many times the desire for the item will be replaced by a more thoughtful, rational decision making process.

3. **Intention:** Learn to ignore the songs of the sirens knowing that they just want to lead you onto the rocks. Leave the credit cards at home.

4. **Be FIT:** Remember your Financial Independence Threshold, the amount of money you set as your goal? Think of debt as an enormous obstacle in your way to reach that goal.

5. **Trade down to wealth:** A smaller home, a less whiz-bangy phone and a less fancy car are all ways you can accelerate your financial goals. Phone plans are just another form of delayed gratification. Add up the total annual cost and use that as your decision-making criteria, not just the monthly amount.

6. **It's not used, it's pre-tested:** Let others test the items you buy (*to make sure they're good*). In other words, try to buy as many things as you can on the

secondary market. Craigslist & garage sales *not* the mall. A bonus is that when you buy used from an individual, you are forced to pay with cash.

Stop incurring new debt. Consumer debt is self-imposed slavery and it is **absolutely critical** to eliminate the debt you have and to never buy with credit again. If you are serious about achieving financial independence, you must get out of debt and stay out of debt by avoiding the sirens.

Enemy Five: Beware the Guru

Experts are everywhere. Experts want to give you tax advice, law advice and especially money advice. We need experts, people who have spent their lives in pursuit of specialized knowledge in one area or another. Surgeons, lawyers, accountants and even politicians can serve many with their expertise. Unfortunately, even among professionals, **misaligned incentives** can make them work against you rather than for you.

Incentives

Steven Levitt, author of **Freakanomics**, argues that it really is all about incentives. If a person gets paid by the hour, expect things to take longer. If that same person gets paid a commission based on results, they may find more motivation to complete the task more quickly. In general, if a system is set up to financially reward one behavior over another, expect to see that rewarded behavior more often. Stock crashes, corruption, cheating and all sorts of bad behavior have their roots in poorly designed incentives.

When incentives are lined up properly, people can be motivated to do amazing things. In most cases, a financial incentive needs to be bolstered with a strong set of guardrails to keep people accountable and on track. Our society depends on professionals serving each other. Knowing the incentives people have will help you make a better decision and there are a few important questions to ask before seeking the counsel of any expert:

1. What are their incentives for working with me? What's in it for them?
2. How do they get paid for helping me? (Sometimes it is obvious, other times it is not.)

Your Best Interest

Who has your best interests in mind? Mom? *Probably.* Dad? *Maybe.* Very few people other people do. You must embrace the knowledge of experts without allowing their specialized training in their particular discipline to generalize. This means simply avoid putting others up on a pedestal. Keep your interests and goals in mind as you seek the guidance of anyone.

Too Good to be True

One of the most intriguing of the five rituals of wealth is to *be your own boss*. While beginning to discover the places you can serve others, you may find yourself evaluating business opportunities that align with your vocation and purpose. Many ventures calling themselves business opportunities are thinly veiled scams designed specifically to bilk the eager entrepreneur. This makes the adage do what you are even more of a necessity. When you are passionate a particular area, you tend to study it more. It is from that study that you will more easily separate the opportunities from the opportunists. These opportunists range from self-minted experts to malicious scammers. Regardless of their intent, the outcome is the same.

Business growth is usually linear in nature. If an opportunity promises enormous, instant profits with minimal effort and risk it is in your best interest to be skeptical. Starting any business will take effort, investment and risk. You must consider both the message and the messenger. Strive to fully understand the motives of the guru who is offering advice.

As you have been reminded several times, you should focus on doing what you are, not just pursuing money.

> **"Chase two rabbits get none."**
>
> **—Russian proverb**

Become your own expert

There are certain areas everyone should strive to become knowledgeable in, even if you do not pursue the disciplines as a career or business. These are things that every American should have a working knowledge of. At the very least, becoming competent in the areas outlined will help you seek the counsel of experts. Again, your local SBA, SBDC offices and SCORE mentor can be a resource for all of these critical areas.

1. **The law:** Ignorantia juris non excusat. "Ignorance of the law excuses no one."
2. **Taxes:** Understand the two tax systems. Keep abreast of changes in tax law that affects your business. Pay no more than your fair share of taxes.
3. **Accounting:** Understand what an Income Statement, Balance Sheet and Cash Flow statements are and how to use them. The SBA is an excellent resource for this fundamental knowledge.
4. **Marketing and communications**: Read **Crush It!** By Gary Vaynerchuk and everything by Seth Godin. Learn how to use social media to get your message out there.

When you summon the courage to do what you are and discover what you love to do in a way that helps others you will more easily accumulate the expertise to distinguish opportunity from fraud. When seeking the counsel of an expert, knowing *"what's in it for them"* will help you make a better decision. Be your own guru.

Seizure

Having mastered the rituals of wealth our hero has discovered that the treasure he sought was within him already. He learned to pay his wealth first, to eliminate the burden of debt and to give graciously to charity. He learned to live frugally and to pay cash for all things. He understands the value in being his own boss by doing what he is and serving others in his own unique way.

Having slayed the enemies of wealth through education, common sense and determination, our hero found more strength within himself than he believed existed. He learned that get rich quick schemes are abundant in a free society and only with diligent research are they held at bay. He learned that a life of conspicuous consumption drains him of power and destroys his chances of ever attaining financial independence. He was able to silence the Sirens of debt and to become his own expert in the areas of finance, law and his chosen business.

At various points along the way it is important to take time to reflect. Especially now in our data-rich, always on world we must carve out chunks of time in order to do nothing. Recreation is time we give to ourselves and is an opportunity to re-create our lives in our mind. It can be a powerful experience to do this on paper. Re-create the past 30 days, the past 6 months, and the past year. Spend some time alone. Turn off the mobile phone and reflect.

It is easy to get consumed with "**Always looking forward**", especially if we associate embarrassment of pain to our mistakes. The art of reflection allows us to acknowledge our mistakes and move forward from them. We usually discover many more triumphs than we have given ourselves credit for as well.

1. *What mistakes have I made over the past few months? In what ways did these turn out to be beneficial?*
2. *What habits or rituals have I adopted?*

3. *Which ones have I eliminated?*
4. *What have I done that I am especially proud of?*

With this treasure in hand it is now time to embark upon...

The Magic Flight

"If the hero in his triumph wins the blessing of the goddess or god ... the final stage of his adventure is supported by all the powers of his supernatural patron. On the other hand, if the trophy has been attained against the opposition of its guardian... then the last stage of the mythological round becomes a lively, often comical, pursuit." (Campbell, The Hero With a Thousand Faces, 1949)

The Magic flight is often characterized by the hero fleeing the innermost cave with the treasure firmly in hand. It is a series of challenges that are thrust upon the hero. These challenges are meant to aid in his her growth. By overcoming these obstacles in succession, our hero develops more confidence, strength and power.

Your competitive advantage

"Are you going to succeed because you return emails a few minutes faster, tweet a bit more often and stay at work an hour longer than anyone else?"

—Seth Godin (from Seth Godin's blog)

Seth Godin, author of Purple Cow

The Competition

In any worthwhile endeavor where there exists a marketplace for our goods or services, there is always competition. If your product or service doesn't have competition there are probably 2 reasons for it:

1. The idea sucks. There is no competition because there is no market for this idea.
2. The idea is fantastic. You are so far ahead of the curve that you have created an entirely new marketplace.

Both scenarios have challenges. If your product sucks people will simply ignore it and buy something else. If it is revolutionary, they won't know **why** they need it. Having competition is good in that it proves that a market of people exist that might be willing to try your product or service.

Seth Godin has become one of the world's foremost marketing experts in recent years. Pick up any book that he has written and I am certain that you will eventually read them all. I highly recommend, in addition to his books, that you subscribe to his blog and follow him on twitter. In a recent blog post, Seth had this to say about people abandoning their idea because of competition:

Two big pieces of news for you:

1. **Competition validates you. It creates a category. It permits the sale to be this or that, not yes or no. And this or that is a much easier sale to make. It also makes decisions about pricing easier, because you have someone to compare against and lean on.**
2. **There are six billion people in the world. Even if your market is hand-made spoke shaves for left-handed woodworkers, there are more people in your market than you can ever hope to track down.** (Godin, Competition, 2010)

Collaboration

Collaboration is when people share learning, knowledge and resources in the pursuit of a common outcome. Game theory calls this type of interaction **non-zero-sum** or **win-win**. There are many types of win-win activities and it really depends on our chosen endeavor how to implement this style. In almost all cases finding a like-minded person who offers a supplemental resource to the marketplace can actually improve our offering. Instead of dividing the pie, we simply bake a bigger one. Even with the same number of slices there is now more pie for everyone.

Paul Zane Pilzer explained in his seminal work, Unlimited Wealth that resources are not as scarce as traditional economists would have us believe. In fact, the very definition of economics, how society deals with limited resources, is part of the problem. When we add the elixir of **technology**, as in the case of a more efficient vehicle, we find that once scarce resources become much more plentiful. He believes that we live in a world of unlimited physical resources because we have the creative capacity to consistently advance our technology and therefore to preserve these critical resources long before we consume them.

There are many new tools that enhance collaboration efforts and enable people from all over the world to work together in pursuit of a common goal.

Creative Drive

Creative drive is a form of effort that encompasses both competition and collaboration. With creative drive, you are working with others and competing with yourself. You are focused on being the best you that you can be for the benefit of others. There will always be real competition for customers in any industry but if you focus more of your effort improving yourself rather than just beating the competition, you will thrive.

Stages of creative drive:

1. Define your outcome! In what capacity do you want to engage in this business and what amount of the market do you want to own?
2. Identify top competitors and the elements of their success. Identify opportunities for collaboration. Areas where you bring specialized knowledge or expertise into the marketplace and can help others in the industry grow.
3. Define your target market and identify the allies you can collaborate with to pursue similar outcomes.
4. Create a product or service that fills a need of your market. When you are doing what you are you can identify opportunities to serve others utilizing your unique talents, skills and passion.

With your growth objectives in place and your competitors identified it is time for...

The Return

Refusal of the Return

"No one realizes how beautiful it is to travel until he comes home and rests his head on his old, familiar pillow."

—Lin Yutang

Coming to grips with your own success, power and responsibility is perhaps the greatest trial of all. We are all powerful; we have immense opportunity to do great things or to do horrible things with our power. As we assume roles of leadership in our lives whether as parent, boss or elected official, we must strive to live in accordance with our values.

"So they crossed the bridge and passed the kill by the river and came right back to Bilbo's own door."

-J.R.R Tolkien (The Hobbit)

Crossing the return threshold from a life changing adventure requires a period of reflection and adjustment. When the first astronauts returned from the moon, NASA was perplexed by their behavior. Instead of being elated they were falling into deep states of depression. Upon further study it became apparent that new outcomes and objectives needed to be established for these men in order to provide for reentry into the Ordinary World. Where do you go after you have been to the moon? What goal would even come close?

When you reach your goals take a moment to celebrate. Ask yourself what challenges you had to deal with in pursuit of this goal. Many times the goal seems inconsequential when compared to the experience of pursuing it. What did you learn? How did you grow?

Crossing the Return Threshold

Money can be a useful benchmark. It can be a useful measuring stick that compares your relative growth and effectiveness to others. If that is **all** it is however, you will likely remain frustrated. As we learned earlier, money is simply a measure of value. With few exceptions, what you spend your money on displays your values to the world. Use the money you earn to assert and support your values. It does not matter what you do and how much money you earn. Achieving financial independence can be done on just about any income level and within any occupation.

"If a man is called to be a streetsweeper, he should sweep streets even as Michelangelo painted, or Beethoven played music, or Shakespeare wrote poetry. He should sweep streets so well that all the hosts of heaven and earth will pause to say, here lived a great streetsweeper who did his job well."

— Martin Luther King Jr.

The Greatest Reward

The hero's greatest reward and what helps make every life worthwhile is contribution. Within each one of us is the need to leverage the unique talents we are born with and skills we develop in the short time we have on this planet to serve others. We must contribute. We must give. Only when we contribute to our family, community, country and world do we expand ourselves and grow.

> **"When you cease to make a contribution, you begin to die."**
>
> **—Eleanor Roosevelt**

One of the most important vehicles for our contribution is charity. **Helping those who need it**. We have discussed in detail that giving is a fundamental ritual of wealth. It is worth repeating. For some people there is a tendency to put off charity until they've 'made it', until they have reached a certain level of success. Unlike some of the other habits that delay our gratification, charity gives us instant feedback.

Charity enriches us and the community the second we engage in it and as with all habits that serve you, start where you are.

> **"If you can't feed a hundred people, then just feed one."**
>
> **—Mother Teresa**

The Short Course

For those of us afflicted with a short attention span it is sometimes helpful to have a summary of everything we covered. The journey to financial independence follows the following stages:

The Ordinary World

The ordinary world is **home** and represents our current life and habits. First we need to take stock of where we are by creating our personal balance sheet tracking our expenses. We learned that we can *change our brain* and that **our habits, not our money, are the key to financial independence.**

The Call to Adventure

Our personal call to adventure is following our bliss. This is the beginning of our journey where we define what wealth means *for us*; learn to listen for our bliss and to **define our purpose**. We learn about what financial independence really means and how we can set goals for our life that are in alignment with our values.

Refusal of the Call

We refuse our call to adventure when we are afraid. Our fears come from the limiting beliefs we have about our abilities. It is at this stage that we eliminate beliefs that hold us back and develop beliefs that serve us.

Meeting with the Mentor

The mentors of myth are the ones who brought wisdom to the hero. We learn to seek out a mentor in our chosen endeavor.

Threshold Guardians

We learn to identify the people or things that stand in our way. We learn that there is no failure, only feedback and the fear of ridicule is not worth the price we pay for it.

The Five Rituals of Wealth

We first take stock of all the ways we are **already wealthy** and then begin learning the five wealth rituals:

Wealth Ritual One: Pay Your Wealth First
Wealth Ritual Two: Be Frugal
Wealth Ritual Three: Be Your Own Boss
Wealth Ritual Four: Cover Your Assets
Wealth Ritual Five: Live with an Attitude of Gratitude

The Road of Trials

At this stage we learn about character, how to fix our regrets and the power of perseverance.

Defeat the Five Enemies of Wealth

In addition to the rituals of wealth we adopt, there are also five insidious wealth destroyers in our lives that we must defeat:

Enemy One: The Fear of Risk
Enemy Two: The Dozers
Enemy Three: The Aspirationals
Enemy Four: The Sirens of Debt
Enemy Five: Beware the Guru

Seizure

Seizing the sword is achievement. It is getting the treasure we seek. At this stage we celebrate our hits, reflect on our misses and review our progress.

The Magic Flight

The magic flight is a series of challenges that the hero goes through after achieving his primary goal. At this stage we discuss our competition, how to collaborate and how to develop creative drive.

The Return

At first, the hero refuses the return to the ordinary world. Developing new habits and reaching goals changes you. Once you cross over, it is important to share the magic elixir you found on your quest with others. The Greatest reward is the joy that contribution brings.

The Shoulders of Giants

I cite several references throughout the journey. In fact, as I mentioned in the introduction, there are no **new** fundamentals. The ideas presented have been thoroughly tested and proven to work. If I had to just pick four authors that have had the most impact on my financial success, I easily come up with this:

Andrew Tobias

Twenty years ago I was in terrible debt, had awful money habits and spent every dollar I earned the moment I got it. I reached a point where I knew I had to do something about it so I went to the bookstore looking for answers (don't ask me why it wasn't a library!). Several hours later, **The Only Investment Guide You'll Ever Need** was the book I walked out of the store with. If you skipped to here and have only a few dollars to purchase a book, put this one down and find the latest edition of Andrew Tobias' epic tome. It is funny, easy to read and full of the best financial advice you'll ever get. I still have my dog-eared original but I have picked up every edition since then. Frugality, prudent investing and avoiding costly mistakes are hallmarks of his financial philosophy. Do yourself a favor and get a copy.

Burton Malkiel

Once my new habits took hold, I decided I was smarter than the market. Since I was so smart, investing in stocks that **I pick** with my **expert analysis** would not be speculative, it would be prudent. It took one book, and *several thousand dollars down the drain* to convince me otherwise. Malkiel is the most famous proponent of the efficient market hypothesis, which says essentially that the stock market has almost all of the publicly available intelligence baked into it and trying to beat the leading indicators is a loser's game. The book I read was **The Random**

Walk Down Wall Street and it changed my life. Fortunately, it is not 100% necessary to read that giant (450+ page) book. A *"what to do"* and *"why to do it"* version exists in **The Elements of Investing,** his latest book (along with Charles Ellis). At 176 pages, it can be read in a day.

Jim Rohn

Jim Rohn is the epitome of the wise old man, the mentor of antiquity. I was fortunate to spend a weekend at one of his live seminars several years ago. He imparts his wisdom without filler, without unnecessary loftiness and without the expectation of buying another book or seminar. I have several of his quotes and portions of his philosophy sprinkled throughout this book. Reading his material does not do it justice, though. He was an excellent orator who honed his delivery for over 40 years. It is worth it to see and hear a seminar or speech expertly delivered by the man himself. I recommend getting the video recording of his **How to Have Your Best Year Ever Seminar**. Experiencing Jim Rohn in this way can really be life-changing.

Anthony Robbins

Stories of Tony Robbins' intensity, skill and commitment to help people change are legendary. Presidents, pro athletes and business people credit Tony with their success. While he has written two excellent books on the subject it is his live seminars and audio programs that I love the most. He truly understands how the human animal works and delivers on his promises. Get a copy of **Ultimate Edge** and prepare to be blown away.

If all you did is pick up **The Only Investment Guide You'll Ever Need, The Elements of Investing, How to Have Your Best Year Ever Seminar** and **The**

Ultimate Edge you will have everything you need to become financially independent in very short order.

THE HERO'S JOURNEY TO FINANCIAL INDEPENDENCE
WILLIAM RADFORD

Bibliography

Baumeister, R. F., & Tierney, J. (2011). *Willpower: Rediscovering the Greatest Human Strength.* Penguin Press.

Botkin, S. (2011). *Lower Your Taxes - Big Time!* McGraw Hill.

Campbell, J. (1949). *The Hero With a Thousand Faces.*

Campbell, J. (1949). *The Hero With a Thousand Faces.* New World Library (2008 Edition Cited).

Columbus, C. (Director). (2001). *Harry Potter and The Sorcerers Stone* [Motion Picture].

Emmons PH.D, R. (2008). Thanks!: How Practicing Gratitude Can Make You Happier. Mariner Books.

Godin, S. (2010, August). *Competition.* Retrieved from seth godins blog: http://sethgodin.typepad.com/seths_blog/2010/08/competition.html

Godin, S. (2011, December). *Your Competitive Advantage.* Retrieved from seth godin's blog: http://sethgodin.typepad.com/seths_blog/2011/11/your-competitive-advantage.html

Graham, B., & Zweig, J. (2011). *The Intelligent Investor.* Collins Business.

Halpern, J. (2010). *Sh*t My Dad Says.* New York: Harper Collins.

Harvard University. (2000). *The Social Capital Cummunity Benchmark Survey.* Retrieved from The Social Capital Cummunity Benchmark Survey: http://www.cfsv.org/communitysurvey/

Jackson, P. (Director). (2012). *The Hobbit* [Motion Picture].

Jackson, P. (Director). (2012). *The Hobbit : An Unexpected Journey* [Motion Picture].

Josephson, M. (2002). Making Ethical Decisions. (p. 34). Josephson Institute of Ethics.

Kahneman, D., & Deaton, A. (2010, Sep 7). *High income improves evaluation of life but not emotional well-being.* Retrieved from PNAS: http://www.pnas.org/content/early/2010 /08/27/1011492107.full.pdf+html?sid=f7f 98964-b5a9-416a-98b1-5745dc8df150

Knutsen, B., Rick, S., Wimmer, G., Drazen, P., & Loewenstein, G. (2007). Neural Predictors of Purchases. *Neuron,* 147-156.

Lucas, G. (Director). (1977). *Star Wars* [Motion Picture].

Lucas, G. (Director). (1977). *Star Wars Episode IV* [Motion Picture].

Malkiel, B. (1973). *A Random Walk Down Wall Street: The Time-tested Strategy for Successful Investing.* NY: W.W. Norton.

Pilzer, P. Z. (n.d.). *Unlimited Wealth.*

Prelec, D., & loewenstein, G. (1998). The red and the black: Mental accounting of savings and debt. *Marketing Science,* 4-28.

Robbins, A. (1992). *Awaken the Giant Within.* Free Press.

Rohn, J. (1999). The Weekend Seminar. Washington DC.

Rohn, J. (n.d.). *How to Have Your Best Year Ever Seminar.* Retrieved from Jim Rohn: http://www.jimrohn.com

Rohn, J. (n.d.). *The Seven Strategies For Wealth and Happiness.* Three Rivers Press.

Schwartz, B. (2005). *Barry Schwartz on the paradox of choice.* Retrieved from TED Talks: http://www.ted.com/talks/barry_schwartz _on_the_paradox_of_choice.html

Schwartz, J. M. (2011). *You Are Not Your Brain : The 4 step Solution.* Avery.

Stanley, T. (2009). *Stop Acting Rich.* Wiley.

Stanley, T., & Danko, W. (n.d.). *The Millionaire Next Door.* Wiley.

Strunk, & White. (n.d.). *The Elements Of Style.*

Thoth, L. (n.d.). *Accurate Pie Chart (original version).* Retrieved from http://tongodeon.livejournal.com/583338. html

Tobias, A. (2010). *The ONLY Investment Guide You'll EVER Need.* Mariner Books.

Vaynerchuk, G. (2009). *Crush It!: Why NOW Is the Time to Cash In on Your Passion.* Harper Studio.